SAY IT ONCE
The No Bullshit Guide to Parenting

SAY IT
ONCE

The No Bullsh.t
Guide to Parenting

KYSA KELLEHER

INKWATER
PRESS

Publisher: Inkwater Press | www.inkwaterpress.com

Paperback
ISBN-13 978-1-62901-388-6 | ISBN-10 1-62901-388-9

Kindle
ISBN-13 978-1-62901-389-3 | ISBN-10 1-62901-389-7

Printed in the U.S.A.

3 5 7 9 10 8 6 4 2

For David, Ian, Teddy, Wiggy, Harvey, EJ and Grady.
I love on ya.

Contents

Disclaimer xv

PART I

My Story

1

Lesson: Making Decisions 6

Lesson: School 14

Lesson: Cooking 15

Lesson: Everyone Does Their Part 18

Lesson: Chores 19

Lesson: Good Manners 21

Lesson: Bodies 27

Lesson: Getting Out 30

Lesson: Passion 31

Lesson: Experiencing Life 35

Lesson: Going For It 40

Lesson: Learning 42

Lesson: Rough Patches 45

Lesson: Creativity 47

Lesson: Consequences 49

Lesson: Sticking to Your Words 50

Lesson: Discipline with Manners 51

Lesson: Really Going For It 53

Lesson: Qualifications 54

Lesson: Work 57

Lesson: Consistency 63

Lesson: Making Time for Yourself 66

Lesson: Taking Care of Yourself 70

Lesson: Accepting Help 70

Lesson: Scheduling 74

Lesson: Sleep 75

Lesson: Opinions 77

Lesson: What Works for Your Family 79

Lesson: Being Prepared 82

Lesson: Don't Sweat the Small Stuff 84

Lesson: Stick with It 86

Lesson: Pause 88

Lesson: Empowering Your Kids 91

Lesson: Traveling with Toys 93

Lesson: Screen Time 93

Lesson: Don't Stress 97

Lesson: Slowing Down 98

Lesson: Speaking Up 100

PART II

Manual

103

Basic Kelleher Rules 105

Feeding You and Your Family 106

Snacks 107

Babies until the age of 2 107

Ages 2 to 4 108

Ages 5 to 11 111

Ages 12 to 20 ... The Growth Spurts 112

Age 20 and Up 112

Serving Your Family Food 113

    Sitting at the Kelleher Table 113

    More Rules About Sitting at the Family Meal Table 115

Lunch 118

Let's Sum Up Feeding Your Family 121

Plain Old Parenting 122

Independence 124

    Toddlers 124

    Ages Four to Nine 126

    Tweens, Ages Nine to Twelve 127

    Teens 128

Getting Up and Out the Door 128

Going to Bed 131

Getting Your Kid a Phone 133

Homework 135

Issues at School 138

Say It Once; Repeat ONLY if Needed 139

Thank You 143

Money 144

Clothing 146

I'm Sorry 152

Pause 154

Be a Polite Parent and Discipline with Manners and
Kindness 157

Deliver Your Punishment in 20 Words or Less 158

Speak Slowly 159

Punishment and Natural Consequences 159

Have a Seat 161

Let Them Tell You ... If They Will 164

Shame 166

Bribe 168

Learning for the Little Ones 173

"You're Okay" 174

Don't Bring a Toy 176

Offer to Help 179

Whispering to Your Kids 182

Let Your Kids Be 183

No Sharing Allowed 184

Sports & Activities & Attitude 186

We Do Not Give Our Children Warnings 187

How to Get Your Kids to Clean Up 189

Don't Cut the Crusts Off Your Kids' Sandwiches ...
and All the Other "Firsts" We Need to Avoid 193

Screaming Kids in the Car 196

Forget ... "Can You" 197

Patience 198

Taking the Kids to Eat in Public 200

Reading Time 202

Sleep 203

Screen Time 207

Kids ... The Morning 208

Your Children's Guests 209

The End 210

The Household 213

Cutting Nails 213

Emergency Contact 213

Plastic Bag 214

Kids' Artwork 215

Thank You, Teachers 216

Kids' Socks 216

There Was Once a Diaper at the Park 217

2 Great Tips for Kids' PJs 217

Alarm Clocks for Kids 218

Double Sheets 220

Kids' Athletic Gear 220

Disposable Cups 220

A Permanent Marker 221

Flip-Flops, Keens, and Crocs 222

Chiffonier, Bureau, Highboy, Dresser, Cabinet,
Wardrobe, Etc. 223

Smoke Detectors 223

Clean Your Car in Public 224

Doctor's Appointments 224

Gesundheit or Salud or Prosit 225

Kids' Medicine 226

No Empty Hands 227

Storing/Organizing Memories 228

Frozen Pizza 229

Vacation and Groceries 230

Speaking of Meal Planning 230

Produce Bags 231

Family Schedule 232

60 Minutes 234

Sprinklers + Soap 235

Live in 30-Minute Increments 235

Book Party 236

The Bin 237

Birthday Door 238

Toothbrushes 239

Mattresses 239

Pillows 239

Silverware and Kitchen Utensil Drawers 240

Food Expiration Dates 240

MCH 240

Acknowledgments 243

Disclaimer

My credentials for writing this book are slim. I don't have any formal education to parent or write. My parenting education has been on-the-job. But I am a parent and a stepparent. And I write how I talk: in partial sentences, with swear words scattered here and there. I am good at communicating, in an accessible way, what I have learned and what we do at our house and how it works. If you want to follow any of the advice in my book, you need to get on board with it, stay on board with it, be strict with following the plans, ignore the cries and screams as you begin to make changes, and most importantly, be loving to your children.

PLEASE NOTE

The book is broken into two sections. The first section is the story of my life. My story starts during my childhood, and by the end of the book, I have six children. Stories about our children are scattered throughout the book and are not always in chronological order. Within my story, you will find *Lesson* sections; these will give you the tools we use in our household to raise our children. The second section of the book is in a tutorial format.

PART I
My Story

My name is Kysa. I would guess you saw that on the cover of the book. I'm sure you wondered how to pronounce it. I am so used to my name being mispronounced that I don't correct people when they screw it up; I haven't for two-and-a-half decades. However, if you are really curious about how to pronounce my name, it's k-EE-sa—like Lisa, with a "K."

My mom named me. My dad really wanted to name me Jamie Michelle, and my grandmother did all the bribing she could to make it happen. My mom won, thank God. The name Jamie Michelle makes me think of high bangs, light-pink leg warmers, and lots of bubblegum smacking. Before I was born, my mom and dad had a family friend, and their daughter's name was Kristina (I have no idea how they spelled it), and they called her Kysa for short. My mom liked the name and used it. After I was born, we had personalized plates on our car with my name on them. Everyone thought "KYSA" referred to a radio station. My name means "kitten" in Finnish. I don't think I'm much like a kitten—more like a tiger. Read on and you can decide for yourself.

When I was about thirteen, I had had it with my name. I wanted it changed. I was gunning for "Sophie." I practiced writing it and saying it and even thought people would like me more if I had a "cool" name. I gathered the courage to tell my mom. I was afraid I was going to hurt her feelings. I remember the moment so well; we were driving to school. I said, "Mom, I want to change my name." Without batting an eyelash or changing the tone of her voice, she said, "Let me look into it." I had my answer the next day; we just had to go down to the courthouse and fill out some paperwork, and I could have the name of my dreams. Soon I would be Sophie Marie Alport. The name was so great. I couldn't wait!

And then I started thinking about it. This is one of the first times I really remember thinking. I know that sounds odd, but think about it, when is the first time you actually remember thinking about something? Yes, I took in information, but I didn't process it. I didn't tumble it around and try to come up with something else. So this really is the first time I actually remember thinking about something, processing it, and coming up with my own thoughts. I didn't really like my name because it was so different. Every time my name got called in class, I would have to correct the teacher, and then it was a few weeks or even months before a teacher pronounced it correctly, if they ever did. Today I give my middle name, "Marie," when we are waiting at a restaurant and I know my name is going to be called. At this point, I just feel bad for someone who looks at my name and is puzzled. Then they blurt out an attempt.

Back to Sophie. As I thought about changing my name, I thought about my parents. I knew nothing about having kids, but I figured that since they chose my name, they must like it. It would probably hurt their feelings if I let my name vanish into thin air. As you can tell from the front of the book, I didn't change my name. But my mom's willingness to let me have the *opportunity* to change my name left a lasting impression on me. Give your kids choices. Not all of them, but a lot of them—a lot.

Our daughter Murphy has already changed her name, but not legally … yet. David (my husband) and I started it, and she has very strongly carried it on. When Murphy was a baby, she wiggled so much, it was sometimes scary to hold her, especially out of the bath when she was wet. So we used to pass her back and forth and say, "Here's Wiggles." Well, "Wiggles" caught on, and then it graduated to "Wiggy." So our cute little Murphy is now Wiggy. If you ask her what her name is, she will tell you Wiggy. Even to this day, it trips me out. Around age four, Wiggy started gymnastics. After the first class, I asked her what her instructor called her. She said, "Wiggy." I said, "How do they know that's your name?" She said, "Because I told them."

Here's the thing that floors me with this. Wiggy used to be very shy—one of those kids you had to peel off of you. But this name thing has really let her blossom. She likes the name Murphy, but she prefers to be called Wiggy. And she knows if she wants that to happen, she needs to speak up—and she does. I'm not that parent who is going to tell all of her instructors, friends, classmates, and the like that she prefers to be called Wiggy. Nope, if she wants a new title, she is going to have to own it. It's not because I don't want to help my kids out; it's because Wiggy is perfectly capable of speaking for herself. She may not always want to. But if she doesn't want to be called Murphy, she knows it's her job to let everyone know. Talk about empowering a young (four-year-old) lady. We haven't gone to court for Wiggy to change her name, and I am not sure that we will … we shall see. But it doesn't make me sad that she doesn't want to be called Murphy. I feel like my mom probably felt—it makes me happy my little girl is thinking for herself.

David and I laugh about it often. Because we *love* the name Murphy. I love yelling, "Murph, time for dinner." I just love the name. Seriously, try it; it's a great name, and to think a little lady is attached to the other end of it is awesome. But often, I get no response, so I have to say, "Wiggy, time for dinner." Oh well …

I know we can't all pick out great nicknames for our children, hope they stick, and then let our kids run around and inform everyone they would like to be called a different name. And I don't think you should put down this book and ask your kids if there is a different name they would like to be called. But we can empower our children to speak up for and make choices for themselves.

LESSON

Making Decisions

My husband and I let our kids decide as much as we can in their lives. Empowering your children is one of the greatest gifts you can give. We started empowering our children at a very young age. Just be aware that you can go too far empowering your children and end up with spoiled brats. So start with the simple decisions: what would they like to wear, what book would they like to read, what park would they like to go to, what kind of ice cream would they like to have? You get the point. These decisions don't make a huge impact on your life. And if you would like to make things easier on yourself, give your kiddos two choices. You are still empowering them, but you are keeping the options to a minimum. And you are giving them their first lessons in decision making. And, remember, once your kiddos make a decision, no matter what it is, do not let them change their minds. Teach them to make decisions, stick with them, and accept the outcomes.

I mentioned that clothing is a great place to allow your kiddo to call the shots. Harvey, our fourth child, has been wearing a pink shirt with ruffled sleeves and a bunny on the front for two years. He loves it. He gets lots of questions about it, and often people comment on how cute my "daughter" is. But he loves that shirt and it looks great on him. And here's the bigger point: since Harvey was two-and-a-half, he has taken off his pajamas put them in the dirty laundry, taken off his diaper and put it in the garbage, used the toilet, and picked out his clothes and put them on—all on his own. And all of this has been done with almost no drama and minimal assistance from David or me. There is not a chance I am going to step in and argue with Harvey's clothing choices. Giving Harvey the freedom to choose his outfit for the day takes the task of dressing him off my task list, and empowers him to decide what he likes to wear, what feels comfortable on his body, and what clothing works in different types of weather. And the best part is that Harvey starts his day with a big accomplishment: he gets dressed all by himself.

All of our kiddos manage their own clothing. They put their dirty clothes in the laundry and they pick out the clothes they will be wearing for the day.

Clothing is a great tool. Your kids can learn so much just from choosing their own clothing. Let them figure out how to dress. Yes, let your children wear shorts in the winter if they want. Let your kids get cold (unless it's freezing outside); they will be fine. I know it's cute to have your daughter's hair bows match the bows on her socks, but would she choose that? Empower your children to make choices and learn the consequences. Let your kiddos choose. Since we let our kids choose their clothing, when we do have to change the clothing rules on them (for a formal event or sickness or anything else), it's really not that big of deal. Here are a few guidelines to clothing decisions:

We have a fancy party to go to, and there is a dress code. My kids know I call the shots. Here's how I do it. I round 'em up and tell them we have a party at the Smiths' and that they need to dress up in their best and that I have the final say in what they wear. There's no crying because my kids are more jacked to go to a party than to worry about what they are wearing. Mind you, I do not dress our kids up in uncomfortable clothes; it's not worth it.

Your son wants to wear a tutu to school. Let him. If you are worried he is going to get made fun of, put that worry out of your head. Let your kids build a wall of self-esteem young. Every day Harvey gets asked by all the boys in his sister's class why he wears his sister's pink light-up shoes. He just lights up the shoes and walks away; he doesn't care.

Your child wants to wear the same clothes he wore yesterday, but they are filthy. A simple, "I'm sorry, those need a quick trip through the wash; they will be ready tomorrow." You need not say more, just keep repeating yourself: "I'm sorry, those need a quick trip through the wash; they will be ready tomorrow." Yes, your child may kick and scream at you; ignore it. The goal is for your child to get dressed. If he is screaming at you but getting dressed, just ignore him. If he refuses to get dressed and you need to be somewhere, don't say a word. Head out the door. If your child cannot be at home alone, put him in the car without his clothes on. Grab a shirt and pants for when he is ready to get dressed. When your child sees what you have picked out, you will probably hear more ranting and raving. Ignore him and just say, "I'm sorry, I thought you would like these clothes." You don't need to say more. Your child lost the opportunity to pick out his clothing because he was throwing a fit. Your child's decision-making was revoked; you laid down the law, and now your child is dressed. No need to discuss it any further.

Your child wants to wear her swimsuit, but she isn't going swimming. In our house, the answer is "no." Swimsuits are not the strongest material, and I don't want to replace a swimsuit because it got ripped on the playground. Plus, it isn't necessary to wear a swimsuit if you aren't swimming. Remember, your kids will try to push the limits at every turn. And that is great! They are testing their boundaries, flexing their muscles; you want to support that, but you also need to guide them.

Your kid doesn't want to wear underwear. Gross. Learn to say "no" to your child. And let your child learn to understand the meaning of "no." Trust me, you want to learn this early or you will be struggling to say "no" to your drunk teenager when he asks you for the keys to your car.

Our kids choose their own haircuts. When Teddy (our third child) was five, he asked the hairdresser to give him a Mohawk. That was his haircut for his first day of kindergarten. A month later, Wiggy had her beautiful, long (down to her booty) hair cut to a bob. Just last month, Harvey had all his curls cut off to a buzz cut. While Ian (my stepson) was at his grade school, he loved to grow his hair out until the school told him to get it cut. We never said a word. Will I be crying if Wiggy dyes her hair hot pink? Oh yes. And I was sad when she had her baby curls whacked off. But we are giving our children choices; we are empowering them, and it's their hair on their bodies; they should get to choose.

As for sports, our kids choose. Recently, Teddy chose gymnastics over basketball with all the boys in his class. I can rest my head at night knowing that kid isn't following others. We empower our kids to be in charge of themselves. Where we can, we let our children choose. Our children choose the books they read, the friends they have, the games they play, the clothes they wear. How else are we going to allow our children to think through decisions? To make decisions? And to see the outcomes of their decisions?

Don't be mistaken: we are not willy-nilly hippie parents letting our children choose everything. Good God, I do not have time for that. We do not let our children choose their bedtimes, their naptimes, their schools, the amount of their allowance, their curfews, whether or not they wear seatbelts. These decisions are set in stone and rarely budged from.

So think about places in your kiddos' lives where you can empower them to have choices. But give yourself two quick rules: one, if your children's decision-making is taking longer than it should, they lose the opportunity to decide; and two, you need to be okay with whatever the decision is. It's simple to accept your child's clothing choices or birthday cake flavor, but you aren't going to accept your six-year-old's choice to have an 11:00 p.m. bedtime.

I heard a story from a friend the other day ... her family goes out to dinner with another family fairly often. That family lets their child choose what the child is going to eat for dinner. This is great at restaurants; it gives your children tons of power. The choices are limited and your children can work on public speaking by placing their own food order. But it's not great if you make your server wait for two minutes while your child is deciding; that's what that particular family allows. Your kiddos will learn very quickly how to start making decisions. And once they make a decision, remember to make sure you have them stick to it.

I talked a little bit about my name; now let's switch gears to my writing. I am horrible at it. Grammar? Forget it … I don't have a clue. For the most part, you should be able to understand my writing; it's straightforward and to the point. But if you are a big grammar junky, and prepositions and complete sentences are your thing, this is *not* the book for you. *I am not kidding.* Even if you want to read this book, you shouldn't—you will not be able to comprehend anything because you will only pay attention to the grammatical errors. And if swearing causes you heartache, please put this book in your Goodwill pile. I have my own style, and it's based on having zero skill in the writing world. So I'm just going to write like I talk and not worry about all the rules, because I don't know them. As for spelling, I can't do that very well either. I find spellcheck very helpful.

So if I can't write, why am I writing a book? Because I want to. I remember being on a flight back from Australia. I was 19 years old. I went on a learning expedition with the University of Oregon. I was supposed to get college credit, but it was such a boondoggle, I never took the time to transfer the useless credits to my various colleges (Southern Oregon University, University of Oregon, Portland State University, Montana State University, and University of Connecticut). Anyway, I was writing in my journal and just letting the pen go and go and go. I must have written for hours, and I just loved the feeling. It was so rewarding and fun to just let the words in my head spill onto the paper. So this book, which I will make sure goes somewhere, has been on my bucket list for 21 years.

If I were you, I might be wondering why I didn't study journalism or literature or something along those lines if I knew so long ago that I wanted to write a book. I do not know.

Oh well ... in my next life I can study words and sentence structure. In the meantime, I'll pop out this book. In case you are curious, I graduated with a degree in Nutrition and Food Service Management from Montana State University— it has been very helpful in raising good eaters.

I grew up in Portland, Oregon. I went to Oregon Episcopal School for a bit, then my parents got divorced and paying for OES wasn't in the cards anymore. Peter (my brother) and I switched to the neighborhood school, Bridlemile. I remember walking into fourth grade; my teacher was Mrs. Fisk. I did not like her. I am sure I was upset about the divorce and having to switch schools. She probably was a great teacher ... sadly, I will never know. I survived switching schools. I did. I'm here today to tell the story. So if you have to switch your children's schools, don't fret. They will stop crying every night after a few months, and then they will begin to make friends. They will do great their second year at their new school. I promise. I can promise this because we had Ian (my stepson) switch schools in fifth grade. He cried every night for two months. It was tough on him and on us. But we all got through it. We handled him gently as he navigated the waters at his new school.

Here's a quick note on schools, because if you are a parent, this topic is *constantly* on your mind. Schools, daycares, nannies—finding the right place for your children is work. Put on your work boots and mix a stiff cocktail because this road can be bumpy and muddy. I don't have the best advice about picking schools. We did not stress ourselves out about them. Currently, all four of our children go to different schools, and we actually pay money for this madness. If you see a grey Suburban honking at you in Northeast Portland, that's probably me trying to get you to speed up so I can get one of our kids to school. Why did we have our children at four different schools? It just worked out this way.

When I had Teddy at home and was pregnant with Wiggy, I remember David's ex-wife, Kristen, telling me she was putting her daughter in school. I was like, what? School? I wondered what she was going to do all day; like me, she didn't work. I mentioned it to David, and he said, "Before you judge, why don't you think about putting Teddy in school." I hadn't even considered it. So I called a few schools around our house and put Teddy on their waiting lists. A month later, a neighborhood school called, and Teddy started school two days a week. I figured if other people sent their kids there, it had to be okay. That was the extent of my research; I figured if I didn't like the school, I would just find a different one or keep him home with me. What was a 16-month-old kid going to learn anyway? I wanted my kids to get sick, try new foods, learn to communicate, and do things for themselves.

Turns out I chose the perfect school for our family, out of luck. The school prepared and served the kids two snacks and lunch from their local farm. Between 7:00 a.m. and 7:00 p.m. they did not care when you dropped your child off or when you picked your child up. It was awesome. Murphy, Harvey, and Teddy all went to this school. When Teddy was two, we signed him up for pre-K at the neighborhood school. When he was old enough, he went there. We didn't really think about it. What can you learn in pre-K? I wanted our kids to learn to communicate, care for themselves, and gain confidence. Teddy had fun in pre-K and learned all his letters and numbers that year.

Here's the thing with education—you can send your child to the best school on the planet, but does that make your child an amazing person? No, it does not. Your children are born with the brain they are born with. Yes, you can teach a child a lot, but you cannot make them smarter. So build character, build confidence, build capable children. And I say "build," because raising children is like building a building ... one brick at a time ... one little experience at a time. If your children are smart (like we all want our kids to be) that's great—it will just naturally unfold. Until you figure that out, just love your children and build them into great people. Try not to stress about creating mini-Einsteins.

LESSON

School

I am sure you have been into or are about to start the rat race of school. The school thing can be crazy and very overwhelming. Everyone has their own story, and if you don't have one yet ... you will. I, of course, have a lot of stories, good and bad. But what it comes down to is thinking about the principles in your family. For our family, we really like to empower our kids and teach them to be self-sufficient. I want a school that will hold our kids accountable and inspire them. I want our children to get excited about learning, experiencing, seeing, and exploring.

So my advice to you is, see what works for your family. See what works for your child. If you are willing to commit to a 45-minute commute each way to get your kiddo to school, go for it. If paying for your child to attend school works for your family, go for it. If the public school is awesome, then that's your place. It's a tough choice and the choice is not always yours. But I would do what works for your family. And don't forget your work boots and a stiff cocktail as you are navigating all this. You'll need it.

Back to me. Grade school was fine. I did the minimum. I remember working on a history project about the Pilgrims with my friend Kathleen Reilly (now Helmer). We were going to cook a "real" Thanksgiving dinner. I did not know my way around the kitchen. At that time, in my family, we were either eating dinner at McDonald's or having cereal at home; my mom was working a lot. So when Kathleen suggested we work together, I thought, great, I know her mom cooks. We went up to her house, where I followed her around the kitchen in shock. She could do it all. She really knew her way around the kitchen, and her mom was right there to lend a hand. Plus, there were seven brothers and sisters to pitch in too if we needed it. It was awesome. It was so fun to be in the kitchen, cooking away, creating, chatting, tasting, and laughing. We really had a blast.

LESSON

Cooking

Learn to cook! Learn your way around any kitchen. I don't mean just make Top Ramen and leave the dishes in the sink. I mean, learn how to make a real meal. If you are cooking for six, learn how to plan a meal for six, purchase a meal for six, cook a meal for six, set a table for six, and clean up a kitchen after a meal for six. By no means do I think everyone needs to be a housewife, but I think every man and woman should know how to prepare a meal. I started cooking with Ian once a week when he was seven. Yes, he hated it, and it was like pulling teeth to get him going. But once we started mixing and chopping and tasting this and that and listening to crazy stories on NPR, he loved it. Ian is not fully ready to prepare a six-course meal, but he is very close.

When the little ones were ages three, four, and five, I started cooking with them in the kitchen. You ask, why didn't she start sooner? I could barely get dinner on the table with four children; adding a cooking lesson into the mix was out of the question. As you read on, you will find I never kill myself to parent these kids. Oh, do I love each of them, but the minute I start trying to be a "super mom," the whole system falls apart.

So I started cooking with Harvey (three years old at the time). We made cauliflower risotto; it was horrible. But Harvey and I had a blast cooking together. He chopped a whole head of cauliflower in the Cuisinart; he cleaned spinach and then tore it up into tiny pieces for a salad. He also mixed up our salad dressing and set the table. He really enjoyed himself. And the more interesting part is that Wiggy and Teddy were begging to help. I only wanted to manage one kid in the kitchen, so I told them they would have to wait for another night. I try to have one of the kids help me with dinner every night. They are not always helping with the entire process, but they can hop in and lend a hand here and there. It's great quality time with my kids; they are learning a ton, and it removes one kid from the mix of possible arguing while I'm trying to get dinner ready. If I keep this up, I know I will be sending six kitchen-capable kids into the world and maybe even a future chef.

And if you think I am crazy for having my kids help me cook—given the mess, the time commitment, and so on—you are thinking about it all wrong. All children love to be with their parents. What a great way to spend time with your kiddos and get something done together. If you could sit at my dinner table while the kiddo who cooked dinner is telling the others about the dinner he made, and then hear the gratitude from the other kids, you wouldn't think twice about preparing your next meal with one of your kids.

One more thing to add here: I let my cooking assistant taste, snack, and try whatever we are making.

When I was growing up, I always helped around the house. When my parents divorced, it was very hard on my mom. The divorce was a huge change for her. We downsized to a rental home. It worked; we all had bedrooms, but it wasn't our old house. I remember a lot of tears and lots of my mom's friends stopping by to help pack or hang out with us. My mom was always so thankful when a friend grabbed a box to pack or took a bunch of stuff to Goodwill. I paid attention and then started to pitch in and help. At age 10, I used to clean the house from top to bottom after school and before my mom got home from work. My mom always came home so tired, and rarely smiling. This seemed to bring that smile back. And at 10 I was capable of dragging the vacuum around, spraying the counters with cleaner and wiping them down, dusting everything, and picking up.

A clean house was important to my mom, and it is important to me today. For me, a clean house gives me such peace of mind. I am always cleaning, always. This morning I saw toothpaste had dripped down the side of the shelf in the bathroom; I cleaned it up. I never walk by something that needs to be cleaned and not clean it, and if I don't have time, I make a note in my calendar to get it done. We have a large family and dogs; if we don't clean regularly, this place turns into a dump in no time.

LESSON

Everyone Does Their Part

I said I clean all the time; well, so do our kids. All the time. School bags are not dumped at the door and jackets are not thrown on the floor when they walk in the house ... except by my husband. My kids are expected to hang up their coats, hang up their bags, clean out their lunch-boxes, and make their lunches the minute we walk in the door from school. I will not stand for, "I'll do it later." I'm okay listening to the whining and moaning, as long as what needs to get done gets done. If someone dumps their stuff to run outside to play, I call them right back in. I ignore the screams and tears and politely say, "You can go play when this is done." And then I repeat it and repeat it and repeat it and repeat it if need be. I just keep my voice calm and my words polite and my focus on the end results.

I have taught all of our children to unload the dish-washer. Sure, they need help putting stuff up high, and I am happy to help. Our children know how to vacuum with the little handheld vacuum. Ian uses the big vacuum and has been taught to clean vents, under furniture, and up high for cobwebs; he even knows how to vacuum our cars out.

All of our children put away their own laundry. Our kids know they need to clean up all forts, art projects, and toys when I ask. If I get a grumble, I offer to help them or tell them to have a seat on the stair; when they are ready to start cleaning, they can get up from the stair. (I'll explain the stair later.) No child in our house is doing the next activity until what the child has been asked to do is done. Eventually, they get bored of hearing my voice and know I am not going to shut up, so they just get the job done. Am I a nag? Yes, but I do my best to use a polite tone rather than a "bitchy" one. And I try to be smart about what I ask our kids to do, and when I ask them to do it.

ANOTHER LESSON

Chores

Here's my real trick for getting all the jobs done around our house—light bulbs changed, cars vacuumed, the garage cleaned out, leaves raked out of the yard, fridge cleaned out, pantry cleaned out, toys sorted, bathrooms cleaned, furniture fixed, holiday decorations organized—I schedule it during our two hours of chores on the weekend. We have two hours of chores every weekend at our house. This does two things. One, I don't have to do every job in our house, and two, our children are learning some of the jobs and responsibilities of a home. It is not rare to see all four of our children out in the rain working in the yard. Our children are capable of helping out and so are yours.

Kids are never too young to help around the house. I'll touch on this a lot more later. But until you get to that part, start thinking about where your kids can help out. Be polite when you ask your kids to help you around the house; you will get so much further.

During my eighth-grade year, my mom and dad decided my manners were horrible. I'm not sure why. I had been yelled at by my dad for years to put my napkin in my lap and chew with my mouth closed. What else was there? A lot. I was sent to an etiquette class. And guess what? Now that I'm an adult, manners are *very* important to me too. So much so, I read Emily Post cover to cover. And I have sent Teddy (our second child) and Ian to etiquette classes. The rest will follow.

I don't enjoy eating meals with people who treat wait staff poorly (yes, that is part of manners), who don't put their napkins in their laps, who don't wait to start eating until everyone has their food, who eat with their mouths open, who don't understand how to hold their utensils, or who don't thank the person who prepared the meal. Most of us eat three meals a day; we should all learn how to do it correctly.

LESSON

Good Manners

Instill good manners in your children. I believe this starts when you teach your children to sit at a table with others, remain at the table, act reasonably, and eat food appropriately. If our children cannot do this, they do not get to stay at the table. They do not get to finish the meal I have prepared. They can have food when the next meal is being served. I do not budge on this rule. My children have missed a lot of meals. And I have seen a lot of tears and heard a lot screams about them being hungry. It is a privilege to have someone prepare food for you. It is even a greater privilege to have food. All of our children can sit down at a meal and stay at the table. They do not need to get up and run around while they eat; they do not need an iPad or TV to entertain them. Our children need to sit at the table politely, enjoy the food and engage in conversation until they are excused from the table.

How did we teach our children to do this? As soon as our children could sit in high chairs, we buckled them in and they joined us for all meals. They did not sit on our laps during meals; they sat safely in their highchairs. They were served small amounts of whatever we were eating (as soon as it was age appropriate). Children learn a lot from watching. And at a very young age, our children learned to sit at the table and eat their meals. To this day, once our children plant their booties in their seats at the table, they are not allowed to get up from the table until they are done eating. If they do decide to get up from the table for anything other than using the restroom, that meal is over.

Their plates are cleared from the table by them or me. Yes, sometimes they cry and scream. I ignore it.

Like most parenting we do around here, it's black and white. It's not mean, but it is strict. I don't need any gray area or negotiating with my children about whether or not they should sit at the table during mealtime when they have misbehaved. It's not a discussion. If you're wondering how many meals our kids miss because of behavior or getting up from the table, I'll tell you. It's a lot. I would guess there is an average of five meals a week missed by poorly behaved children in our home. Slowly, it's becoming less and less. If your children don't stay at the table or if they misbehave during every mealtime, it is because they do not have consequences for their behavior. Lay down the law and then stick to it. You will start enjoying family meals. And if you are curious why you should sit down and have family meals, look up the stats. I can't remember them perfectly, but sitting down to family dinners decreases the incidence of drug use and obesity, and increases grades. Seems like it's worth it to me.

How do you actually get your children to stay at the table during a meal? First of all, you sit down with your children during the meal and you stay at the table during the meal. And then you keep your little ones strapped into highchairs until you can't squeeze them in there any longer. Our little ones are growing up seeing us sit at the table while we are eating. We don't scream, we don't cry, we aren't on our phones; we actually sit there and talk to and enjoy each other. If you have gotten to a place in your family where the highchairs are gone and your kids won't stay at the table, use a belt. No, don't whip your kids—Jesus! Strap them into their chairs. You did it when they were babies to keep them safe and you do it in the car; now you need to do it to re-teach them to stay at the table. You see, the whole reason your kids "need" to run around while they should be eating is because you let them. And if you think your child needs to run around during a 30-minute meal, you are wrong. I keep a laminated sheet of our table rules on the table. Those who can read love to read it out loud while they are waiting for everyone to be seated. Our table rules are getting cemented in our children's heads because they hear or read them at least once a day.

Observe your kids at school one day. They can probably sit for an hour quietly, having their snack and doing their schoolwork. You know why they can do that? Because their teachers demand it. And you as parents need to start demanding it out of your kids too. Your children can, should, and will sit at a table and enjoy meals with you. If they cannot do that, take their plates away and send them away from the table. Tell them you will serve them at the next meal. Get ready for the tears and screams. But also get ready for a future of relaxing meals with your children. And don't worry, your kids won't starve; they might be a little extra sleepy at bedtime because they haven't eaten. Ignore the crying and pleading. Your children will be fine. They will. And you will be teaching and showing them who is in charge. Because if you have to teach your seven- or nine-year-old this lesson, my guess is you have lost a little bit of the authority in your home. Time to get it back before you have teenagers.

Once you get your kids to sit at the table, start working on manners: the basics for your household. In our house I am working on getting the children to chew with their mouths closed, to not slurp their drinks (even though they love doing it), to use the appropriate silverware for the meal, to put their napkins in their laps, to not scream or sing at the table, and to simply enjoy each other's company. I keep a basket of napkins at the table—so they are on hand for spills and so our children don't wipe messy hands or faces on their clothing.

As I mentioned above, I studied nutrition in college, so I know what I am talking about here ... pay attention. Here is the main rule to get you started: Do not feed your children "kids' food" and yourself something tasty and healthy. Everyone under your roof eats the same food (of course, with the exception of dietary restrictions).

Our children eat everything and try everything. I'll tell you a little story about Ian. I'll also tell you I do not believe in picky eaters. I believe they are created by parents who needlessly cater to young palates. When I started dating David, Ian had a very limited palate. He ate pasta with butter, red peppers, eggs, bacon, and Oreos. And everyone served him these foods. So there really wasn't much of an issue. When I moved in with David, I was excited to cook for a family. I remember the first meal I cooked for us. I picked up Ian and a friend from school and we went back to our house. I was going to make lasagna. The kids were happy playing and I was happy cooking.

When dinner was ready, I called everyone in for dinner. Ian saw what I cooked and the tears started rolling. David started to panic and said in front of Ian, "Ian can't eat that." I knew what the problem was: Ian didn't want to try a new food. Being the bitch that I am, I asked if Ian was allergic to lasagna. David was not happy with my question. Of course Ian was not allergic to lasagna. Ian's friend sat down and grubbed on the lasagna; so did I. David was upset because

Ian was scared to eat and they were at a time where the divorce was brand new. And the girlfriend, me, was brand new too. Disrupting Ian seemed like it would damage him, even if it was just serving lasagna. (My parents did the same stuff when they got divorced. It's funny, everyone says kids are so resilient, but when it comes to divorce, everyone tip-toes around the kids.) But as the tears dried up, David ate and Ian played with his food and took a few bites. To his surprise, Ian survived dinner. That evening, David and I had it out. David is pretty smart—okay, very smart—which is tough for me, because I lose most of our fights with my temper. But that night, I won; it's hard to argue with a nutritionist about serving a child a healthy meal. I set Ian and David straight that night. In our new family, we would not be catering to Ian's limited palate. Instead, we would be enjoying healthy foods together.

Today Ian will eat anything. It took a lot of patient dinners to nudge him to try new foods. I never shamed him into eating. I just put small portions on his plate every night and slowly, very slowly, he began to try everything. That's how you do it, folks. It's very simple. Don't worry if your children only try one bite. That's okay. They are doing two great things: one, they are trying foods, and two, they are listening to their bodies. Little kids are not always hungry. Teach your children early how to feed their bodies. The only way they can do that is if they listen to their little hunger meters. If one bite works for your child, fine. I know it's hard to watch your child only eat one bite and know they won't have food until the morning. But people go for days without food and they are fine. Don't worry. Focus on sitting down to the table to enjoy your family and hear about everyone's day, and let the food be part of the program, not the main subject. You are at the table to nourish your body, not fight with your family about cleaning their plates.

Now that Ian is growing, he practically licks his plate clean, even if he doesn't like the food, because he is so hungry. Ian isn't scared of food anymore. We were gentle with him when he was venturing out and trying new foods. Be gentle with your children, and in about four to five years, they might actually eat an entire meal.

The other night, Teddy had baseball practice, and I decided to the take Harvey and Murphy to dinner. I wanted to go to a Mexican restaurant nearby, but it turned out they didn't allow minors. So we had to go one door down to another place—not a kid-friendly establishment. This place is a "French-Arabesque restaurant serving authentic representations of Middle Eastern dishes." I got that description online. My point is, I took three- and four-year-olds there for dinner. We sat down and I ordered a variety of foods for us all to try. My kids were hungry and they tried all the food. They were not fans of everything, but they tried it all. That's what you are shooting for, folks.

High school was a trip. I had my first kiss in grade school, and now in high school everyone was talking about sex. My mom was always open with us about sex. She talked about it; she laughed when we said "gross." She was very open about it *all*. When I got my period, she was super relaxed about it. My mom took me into her bathroom and cut a panty liner in half. She told me to wear that and change it when I went to bathroom. She explained that I would get my period every month. She got me this pretty little purse to carry my new girly goodies in. My mom had a very open dialogue with us about our bodies. Farting and pooping were hilarious in our family. Sitting on the couch and fanning a fart to your neighbor or rolling up your window in the car after you farted or asking someone to check out this huge bug so they would walk right into your wall of gas made everyone laugh. No, farting doesn't represent good manners, but it opens the door to openly talking about our bodies and having a good laugh.

I think it's high time to get really open with your kids about their bodies. Use your children's age-appropriate terminology and get the conversation going in your home.

LESSON

Bodies

I bought Ian condoms in eighth grade. As I mentioned above, Ian is my stepson. Who's the evil stepmom now? Ian is very funny, and getting funnier and funnier. When I handed him the condoms, he looked me straight in the eye, and without missing a beat, he said,

"Thanks, I needed these."

I of course about fell over. "IAN," I screamed, "Jesus."

He just laughed.

I said, "You have to practice putting it on."

He flipped around, "What!"

I said, "Do you want your first experience to be in the dark with a naked girl trying to wrap it up before the big deed? Trust me, it's impossible."

So I had him go downstairs and he and David put condoms on bananas in the kitchen. Then Ian whipped off the condom and ate his banana. That kid! I am trying to instill the same relationship about our kids' bodies as my mom had with us. I am pretty sure Ian and David will not forget their night of bananas and condoms. And I was so proud of David; he even explained to Ian why you needed to put the condom on right so it would roll down easily and there was a pocket for the sperm. This is huge leaps and bounds for David.

David can't talk about sex. Behind closed doors you would never know this, but it's true. It took me an entire year of nagging and arguing with him to get him to read- *Where Did I Come From?* and *What's Happening to Me?* with Ian. And when I say an entire year, I'm not kidding. And when David and I argue, the gloves come off. A little insight into David and me, he has spent many nights at local hotels because I have asked him to leave. David and I have a good laugh if he has made it through a fiscal quarter sleeping in our bed every night.

Anyway, I finally got my way with David and Ian's sex talk when I dropped this bomb: "Would you like Ian's lasting memories of his sex talk to be with his stepmom explaining that he would get hair on his balls and that he would start getting boners? Or with his father?" David took the books and stormed out. After the talk, David was so proud; he said Ian was awesome and had questions. Now David parades around about this book, and I think he has even bought a few copies for friends. David is slowly learning I am rarely wrong.

There is a lot of joking about bodies in our house. Our boys seem to constantly have their hands down their pants. I say, go for it boys, but not in front of your mom. We all laugh. Murphy wants to get a bra like mine. We talk in our family and we laugh about our bodies. No topic is off limits. So when we need to talk seriously about our bodies, it's not uncomfortable. That being said, last year we started giving Ian a few minutes alone with our family physician. If there is something he wants to talk about, he is learning he can also ask doctors anything. And doctors generally have a few things they want to say to young teenage boys and girls.

We all have fun laughing about penises, vaginas, farting, pooping, and how Wiggy looks like she has a bottom in the front. We also talk seriously about who is allowed to touch their bodies. We say it at the doctor; we say it when we have a new sitter or nanny. We talk about it often. Our children know who is allowed to touch their bodies and who is not. My goal is to make sure that when my kids need anything or have any questions about their bodies, they feel comfortable coming to me or David, because no subject is off limits.

High school was fun. I skied and played volleyball. I was good at both. Volleyball taught me sportsmanship. Skiing taught me to work hard. God, did we work hard. They trained us so hard off the snow we could barely walk after our workouts. On the hill, it was no different. Oftentimes, we weren't allowed to take the chairlift; we hiked to ski. Oregon skiing is no picnic; we weren't wiping snow off our goggles, it was rain. We all had little squeegees on our gloves. Skiing is expensive. I used to get hand-me-down ski gear; I also sold Christmas wreaths door to door every year, and worked at a local ski shop and deli afterschool and on the weekends to cover other expenses.

LESSON

Getting Out

I think kids should work. I think kids should be out in the community, seeing what's out there. They should have someone other than their teachers, coaches, or parents in charge some of the time. I don't think you can realize your dreams and what the world has to offer in the comforts of home, grade school, and high school. I think kids should have the opportunity to be out and about. The summer after eighth grade, Ian got an internship at the Oregon Chapter of the Multiple Sclerosis Society. He worked three days a week. The first day he was in tears, he was so mad. Actually, he went most days in tears or mad that summer. But if he wasn't doing that internship, he would be sleeping until 1:00 p.m. every day. Sleeping in is great, but it's not necessary every day.

So when your kids are old enough, assist them in getting a little summer gig. Ian didn't get paid. We considered paying him ourselves. But in the end, we decided it was okay for him to contribute his time to an organization very near and dear to our family's hearts. David was diagnosed with multiple sclerosis over two decades ago. Ian got rave reviews about his attitude, his smarts, and his work ethic that summer. He gained a lot of confidence. We threw Ian to the wolves (not literally, because the folks at the MS society are like family to us). But Ian was in a completely foreign world. Ian would tell you he would have rather slept in and hung out with friends that summer, but he understands the only way he is going to have anything to put on his college resume is if he goes out and does it! He also understands these experiences are going to help him decide what he wants to do with his life.

I graduated from high school in 1991; I'm 41 years old and counting. I always figured I would go to college, but when it was time to figure that all out, my future was not bright. My grades were marginal. I think I had a 2.7 GPA. High school was crazy. My dad had remarried and had a son; my stepmom wasn't interested in my brother and me. And my brother wasn't happy about the divorce. My friends, skiing, and volleyball kept me sane. My grades weren't really important to me. School wasn't interesting. I didn't have anyone checking on my homework or asking me about school. My brother was having a lot of trouble, and my parents were very focused on him, as they should have been. So I went to school because that's where I was supposed to be. Out of all my high school classes, I remember one teacher, my biology teacher. She was amazing. Other than that, I did not get inspired in high school. I did not learn to study, I did not find my personal interests, and I didn't care about my grades. I was just there in class because that's where I was supposed to be. Thankfully I learned all those lessons later.

LESSON

Passion

Of course I want our children to get good grades. Let's face it, it just makes life easier. But, more importantly, I want our children to be inspired to learn. Inspired to find the "thing" that makes them tick. I want them to find a healthy passion in life. I recently watched a show about grooming standard poodles into various animals and shapes. Yes, it was very funny to see the dogs dyed hot pink and then transformed into a flower or a lion. But what I always love to see in anyone is a passion for something. That is living. When my mom was dying of appendix cancer, she had nothing to do. She didn't have a passion outside of work. As she lay around day after day, reeling from the effects of chemo, there was nothing for her to do. She picked up a few hobbies, but nothing she really cared for. Now, if my mom had been a competitive dog groomer, she could have watched shows about it on TV, read books, and had something to be passionate about. It was sad to watch my mom die, obviously. But it was really sad because it seemed like she had nothing to fill her days. As long as your passion is healthy, no matter what it is, you will have a fabulous, fulfilling life. David and I talk a lot about helping our children find their passions.

Years ago I took the kids to a Lego competition. This young guy, he was probably 26, offered to let Teddy hold one of his personal Lego designs. It was a two-foot sword with a sheath. Teddy was so proud holding it and the guy was so happy to see the smile on Teddy's face. Then the young man offered to let Harvey hold the huge two-foot sword. Harvey was so excited. Then the young man explained how he made a model of his cat out of Legos and the eyes lit up just like a real cat's do in the evening. Sure, we can all laugh about this young man making a Lego replica of his cat. But think about it as a passion and hobby this guy has. He was so proud, so excited to talk about his creations, so full of life. No matter what it is (except of course if it is illegal), I would love for all of our children to find their passions. Someone in this young man's life supported his passions. He was so proud to talk about his Lego sword and Lego cat. I want our children to find their passions and hopefully have the same pride and drive that this young man had.

So help your children find inspiration, help them find their passions. If your kiddo wants to go to beauty school after high school, don't poo-poo it ... think of Paul Mitchell. If beauty is your child's passion, trust me, she will go far. If your child wants to be a mechanic, think about Les Schwab; he built an amazing company. And I'm not saying every child has to build a million-dollar company. No, what I am saying is, if your child is allowed to follow his healthy passion, he will live a fulfilling life.

Let's face it, as parents we want to see our children happy and be able to put food on their tables, take great vacations, and live the lives they want ... and that isn't free. So when I look back on high school, I wish I had been inspired to learn, to create, and to find my way. Thankfully, I found all these things later in life. But I have a few friends who didn't, and they are constantly chasing their tails to find something to fulfill their lives. I have other friends who live vicariously through their children because they didn't live the life they wanted. Help your kids find their passions.

Don't spoil your children with Legos because they love Legos; take them to Lego conventions. Don't buy your child every instrument because they like music; take them to concerts, crank up the music and dance with them, splurge for lessons. If your children have a passion for something, give them experiences to enjoy and learn about. You don't have to spend a fortune to help your children discover their passions; you just have to be supportive and search for options that work for your family.

I went to college in southern Oregon. It was fine. I skied for them and that was fun ... too much fun. I got a 0.9 GPA my first semester—oops! I did a little bit better the following semester, but not by much. That summer I lived at home and tried to clean up my grades at Portland State University, taking anatomy and physiology. That was a flop. I passed, but I had bad grades again. I went back to school in Ashland and lived off campus with some friends. We had a blast, and I did a little better in college, but not much. One night, a friend of mine, Molly, was going to a seminar about traveling to Australia and New Zealand for a few months.

Two weeks later, I left Ashland, went back to Portland, and got a job to raise money for my departure to the other side of the planet. I had traveled a little bit, but not like this. We traveled with 20 other college students to Australia and New Zealand. We traveled with only our backpacks. We did everything during our travels, sky diving, bungee jumping, glacier hiking, backpacking, trying different foods, staying in all sorts of places, scuba diving, snorkeling, sailing, spelunking, etc. We did it all. At age 19, I was crossing things off a bucket list I hadn't even composed yet. I was fearless. My parents were a 22-hour plane ride away. I was free and in charge of myself—it was awesome.

I was starting to learn I could do anything I put my mind to. I wanted to go to Australia and New Zealand, and all I had to do was fill out the paperwork, make some money, and go. I want our kids to have dreams and go for it. I don't want our children to think anything is out of their reach. When I was 25 years old, I got a job at Enron; two days into the job, I wanted to trade energy; and two months into the job, I was trading energy. All I had was a desire, and then I worked my tail off to make it happen. I want to instill that type of drive and passion in our children.

LESSONS

Experiencing Life

Sure, you can't send your five-year-old abroad, but you can send your fifteen-year-old. Take every opportunity you can to step back and allow your children to experience life. Big or small, let your kids live, let them fail, and let them succeed.

Every time we allow our child to take over a job we have been doing for them is a win-win-win (yes, three wins). The first win is because our children are gaining great experiences and the confidence that they are capable and can manage. I could not have accomplished what I have accomplished if I did not have faith in myself. The second win is because anything our children can do for themselves takes work off our plate. And the third win is because when our children leave the nest, we will be sad and scared, but we won't be overly overwhelmed with concerns about them being able to make it on their own, because we have been letting them do things on their own for a very, very long time. We have given our children a lot of challenges while under our roof, and we have watched them figure it out, helped them succeed, or seen them fail. They know what each scenario feels like.

We give our children opportunities to fail. We do not protect our children from failure. Every successful person has had numerous failures. And those who can fail success-fully will succeed. If I was afraid to fail, I would have not applied for the Enron job.

When I returned from Australia and New Zealand, life turned into a huge party. I didn't know what I wanted to study, I didn't know where, and I didn't have a clue what to do. My parents didn't really say much, except that I had to pay my own way. Off I went to shack up with the some friends in Sun Valley, Idaho. It was spring in Sun Valley; skiing was almost over. The town was thinning out from winter tourists, but it was gearing up for summer, and jobs were everywhere. I landed a job painting houses. I had zero experience. Painting is easy once you learn, but you have to be willing to climb ladders and scaffolding like a monkey.

I started the next day. Life was awesome. I spent Monday through Friday painting houses with a bunch of kids from all over the country. Then I would get on my mountain bike and go riding for a few hours with friends in the evening. Then we would swim in whatever pool we could find—this worked awesomely because it got all the paint off. After that, we all went out. I was only 19 years old, but I had scored a fake ID while I lived in Ashland. It was an Oregon ID that would have landed me in jail in Oregon because the guy who made it got busted. But in Sun Valley, it worked like a charm. After a few weeks, I was no longer carded at any of the bars in town.

During that summer, I don't remember buying groceries once. I made enough money to pay rent and bills and to feed myself at various places around town. The only big expense I had was maintenance on my mountain bike. But I could usually find someone to help me with that. That time in my life was so, so, so fun. I really had the life. I didn't pick up a book or expand my mind, intellectually, in any way. But I enjoyed the outdoors. Every weekend was spent hiking, river rafting, camping, or traveling around Idaho, Montana, and Wyoming. I still have a handful of great friends in Sun Valley and others who have moved around the country. We were all there doing the same thing, just enjoying life. It was awesome. I hope all of our children make time in their lives for a similar experience.

With all my fun that summer, I also got a boyfriend. He was a river guide on the Middle Fork of the Salmon River out of Stanley, Idaho. So not only was I now mountain biking, I could go river rafting whenever I wanted. Life was getting better and better. Over the summer, my boyfriend and I decided to move to the Rustler Lodge in Utah. We could live and work at the lodge, and ski on our days off. If you know anything about Utah skiing, you know the state rarely lacks snow, and there are tons of places to ski. Again, I was living the dream. I had my boyfriend at my side, the snow was falling, and life was awesome.

One morning, we got up early and hiked up in four feet of fresh snow. My second turn, I heard a pop and then another pop. My knee was toast. I couldn't ski down; I had to hike, slide, scoot down to the resort to get ski patrol. I saw three orthopedic surgeons and none of them could confirm my knee was hurt. They all asked me over and over again if I was sure I heard it pop. You see, my legs were so big and strong from a summer of mountain biking that the doctors' physical tests weren't working to confirm my injury.

I knew my winter was over. I moved back home and in with my mom, and finally had surgery a month later to repair my anterior cruciate ligament. My surgery went great, but I grew scar tissue at an alarming rate. After three days a week of physical therapy, living with my mom, and having no money, I was fed up. I borrowed a few bucks from my dad and left for Sun Valley. I got there late one night and tracked down my boyfriend. To my surprise, he had moved on to another love interest. I spent the evening crying at a friend's house. The next morning, I woke up. I had to get myself together; I needed a plan. Through the tears I did some good thinking. I knew I wanted to study nutrition; I had heard long ago that Montana State University offered a program. Also, I thought I had a friend from Ashland who had moved to Bozeman, Montana. I remembered seeing a postcard from him on a friend's fridge when I was visiting Ashland during my knee surgery recovery. Remember, this was before the Internet, cell phones, or email. I was able to make a few phone calls via landline (and leave my friends a few bucks for the phone bill). A few hours later, I was talking to Phil on the phone. He was in Bozeman, Montana. He was about to move out of his room and was looking for someone to rent it. Bingo! He said the house he lived in was across the street from Bridger Bowl. The rent was reasonable; I said I would take it. Phil wasn't moving out for a few weeks, but said I could sleep in the living room on the floor until he moved out.

After some goodbyes, I was on my way to Bozeman. I called my dad before I left Sun Valley to tell him of my plans. My dad was excited for me to live in Bozeman, but would not foot the bill for out-of-state college tuition. No problem,

I said: I would get a job and file for in-state residency later; I vaguely knew what I was talking about. After a six-hour car ride, I was knocking on Phil's door. As I was waiting for someone to answer, I heard my name and turned around. Tim was standing there. Tim and I had ski raced together in high school. He lived on the property in the guest house with his girlfriend. Things were looking up. I knew two people in Bozeman and I had only been there five minutes.

The next day, I hit Main Street in Bozeman, hunting for a job. I was thankful this was not my first time looking for a job. I knew the routine: search the want ads in the paper, call for interviews, get an interview, and then call the day after to see if they had made any decisions. I limped into every store and restaurant inquiring about a job. Oh, I forgot to mention: my knee was in horrible shape from the surgery. It was permanently bent, and because of that, that leg was two inches shorter than my other leg. So while I was hunting for a job, I was also interviewing new physical therapists so I could get back to healing my knee. After a few weeks of pounding the streets and calling everywhere in town (using the phone book and a landline and newspapers), I had not found a job. I decided to call a temp agency. Guess who was looking for someone to help in their mail room? Patagonia.

Long ago, Patagonia had their customer service phone center (the folks who answered the phone when you wanted to order from the catalog) in Bozeman. They needed someone to mail out all those catalogs. I interviewed and got the job. It was 40 hours a week as a temp. The clock (12 months) had officially started for my in-state residency. Christmas was approaching, and the Patagonia customer service manager was looking for more reps to manage the phones during the holiday rush. Of course I applied, and I got the job. After the holidays, I was hired by Patagonia as a full-time employee. The job was a blast. We were all working there and going to school and playing outside. Montana is a natural wonderland. There was never, ever a time at Patagonia when I couldn't tag along with someone going on an awesome adventure.

LESSON

Going For It

Teach your children how to go after something. No, don't do it for them. But learn to be a guide for your children. It was my father who suggested the temp agency when I couldn't find a job in Bozeman. It was my dad who told me to ask the customer service manager for a permanent job at Patagonia. It was me who decided to go to Sun Valley; it was me who moved to Utah. I had no fear to go after what I wanted. I still have no fear to go after what I want. Teach your child to figure out what he wants and then lead him in the direction to get what he wants. As you read on, you will see I busted my tail at almost every turn to get what I wanted, and I always have gotten it. My husband and I talk a lot about how both of us have never really not gotten what we wanted. We both believe there is always a way. We both have worked hard to get what we wanted. Teach your children to always GO FOR IT! Lead by example. If there is a dream or something on your bucket list, GO FOR IT. Yes, oh yes there have been failures along the way for me, and for David as well, but we both have always pushed on through.

When Teddy was four, he really wanted to go to golf camp. So I called the local golf course and inquired about their summer camp. Kids had to be six to be in the camp. I signed Teddy up and lied about his age. The first day of camp, I sat in the parking lot to make sure Teddy was okay. Then for the rest of the week, I hung out at friend's house a mile away in case the camp called. Teddy loved the camp. Teddy realized he was the youngest kid at the camp and even got a parting award for it. He has not let his age intimidate him from trying new things. I don't suggest always lying to get what you want for yourself or your children—but I do suggest pushing the envelope a little bit. Life is way too short to follow every single rule.

My twelve months to get residency in Montana finished up right as Patagonia was building their new headquarters in Reno. I was offered a job to move with Patagonia. I was offered moving expenses and a large salary. Remember, I was only 20 years old. It was a big decision, but I didn't want to live in Reno. I was still very close to my friends in Sun Valley, and packing up and moving to Bozeman when my heart was shattered from my ended relationship still had me reeling. My knee was okay, not great, and I had found a physical therapist that was working with me four days a week and not charging me full price. I had started making a lot of friends in Bozeman, so I decided to enter school in the fall as a nutrition student. I didn't give much thought to my previous college grades. But I knew I wanted to graduate from college, so I figured I should get started.

I enrolled at Montana State University with a declared degree in nutrition. At the same time, I started dating a guy named Mark. He was an engineering student and he had to study all the time. I had no clue how to study or that I needed to. But I wanted to hang out with Mark. One night we were in the library and I was staring at the wall while he was plugging away studying. I asked him what he was doing. He was rewriting his notes from that day's lecture and using his book to firm up his notes. I decided to try it; it was better than sitting there trying to look studious. It was incredible! After a few days of this, I realized I understood everything in my lectures. I could actually answer questions in class. Everything clicked. When I took the first chemistry exam, I blew the curve. I was the hated student and I loved it. My grades came out and were sent to my dad in Portland. He called, furious. He screamed at me that I was cheating in school. I told him I was studying for my classes, and he said, "Wow, there *is* a brain in there."

LESSON

Learning

Make sure your kids know how they learn. Do they do best writing everything down? Are they better with flash cards? Should they be quizzed for exams? Do they need to study in a quiet environment? You will not get these answers overnight, or in a year. But check in with your children from time to time and ask them how they learn. Ask them what their favorite subjects are? And why? Help your children discover their dislikes, likes, difficulties, and triumphs in school. No, don't do their homework for them—but from time to time, see what they are up to and what they are studying.

The other night I was quizzing Ian on his biology homework. He was telling me that he remembers the last portion of everything. If I were to give him a grocery list that contained black beans, Twinkies, OJ, apples, and shampoo, he would have to call from the store because he could only remember the apples and shampoo. This might sound bad for Ian, but he's fine. His first semester as a freshman his GPA was 4.47. He knows how he needs to learn. He knows it so well that he knows what he will remember on anything. Make sure you children understand how their brain picks things up, because we all do it differently.

I stayed in Bozeman for two years and then Mark graduated. He got a job back in Massachusetts. I thought he was the one and I wanted to follow him to the East Coast for my junior year of school. I found a program called the National Student Exchange (NSE) Program. I could go to a school that would accept me and continue to work on my degree, with all of my credits transferring back to Montana so I could still graduate on time. After a few months of researching and applying to schools within the NSE program, I was able to start at the University of Connecticut in the fall of my junior year.

UConn did not go well. Mark and I broke up, and that's when I learned about depression. I couldn't get out of bed. I felt like I was living in a hallway and the hallway kept closing in on me. The walls were falling in. I was having cold sweats. I would get really pale. I had to leave class all the time. I was seeing a doctor daily at the student health center. She thought I may have a tumor and set me up for a CAT scan in Hartford. A day before my appointment, I went to her office in a cold sweat and shaking; I knew she would leave a patient to see me if I needed her. I asked her if she thought I was having panic attacks. She sent me downstairs to the school shrink. I was seen right away. I told him my story.

I had moved from Bozeman and was living with 18-year-olds in the dorms (I was in my early 20s). I had joined the ski team, but a terrible skiing accident tore a hole through my calf muscle, and I couldn't ski for the rest of the season and hadn't really made any friends. The shrink said, "You have situational depression." I said, "Can I get some meds?" He said, "Absolutely not. You obviously have a good head on your shoulders, but sometimes life just sucks. And right now, life sucks for you." And boy did life suck.

I was at a great university. The professors at UConn were very interesting and engaging. The facilities were amazing, and one of my closest friends, Teresa, lived in Boston. So life was okay, but I was feeling very low. I was so scared to be labeled with depression and I didn't really understand what it meant. So what else do you do when you don't understand something? Well, back then you check a book out at the library. It took me a week to muster up the energy to go to the library and look for books. I read a book about depression and got a handle on what was happening to me and how long I would feel this way—three months to ten years. Great. I also read a book about natural remedies for depression. I practically started mainlining St. John's Wort. After a few weeks, I started to come out of the clouds. I was still depressed, but the panic attacks were subsiding.

I took one day at a time. If I could muster the energy to go to class, I would. My grades suffered terribly. As I started to come out of my funk and as the panic attacks started to disappear, I realized I was doing more and more. I learned during that year at UConn to take very good care of myself. Now I feed my body what it wants, sleep when I need to sleep, and get all of my chores (laundry, dishes, cleaning, errands, etc.) completed on a daily basis, because all of this stuff fuels my soul. I have always enjoyed exercise, but I do best when it's done first thing in the morning.

LESSON

Rough Patches

Get ready: your kids are gonna go through some major rough patches. Learn to take really good care of yourself for three reasons. One, because you should want to take good care of yourself. Two, because modeling good self-care will teach your children to do the same for themselves. And three, when your kids are having difficult times, you need to be the best parent you can be. My difficult year at UConn taught me to take care of myself. It taught me to listen to myself and my needs. I learned to fulfill my needs. I learned to put myself first.

David and I haven't gone through any major rough patches with these kids yet. But in the first year of our marriage, I started a new job and then quit it, we bought a new house, I was pregnant, I had a baby, and my mom and grandfather passed away, as well as David's grandfather. That was a tough year. I made it through with a lot of love from David and friends, and I had a lot of love for myself.

Our marriage is strong. We fight a lot, but we laugh more. We do things together and we support each other. We know we are doing the best we can to take care of ourselves. David and I come before our children. We are the ones who keep this family ticking. So all of our needs are met before the kids'.

I get up at 4:00 a.m. every morning to get things done around the house. By 5:00 a.m. I am exercising. I have learned this is best for me. No one interrupts my chores or workouts, and I start my days on the right foot. Learn what you need for yourself so you can be the best you can be. If taking a bath is your thing, do it every day. If a glass of wine is the ticket, go for it. Whatever it is, do it. Give yourself that gift, whatever it may be, every day.

Part of my nutrition degree was to do a three-month internship in a hospital. My professor from Montana was supposed to set up all our internships, but I didn't like her style. She had been working the same nutrition internship programs for years. I had not ever heard anything good about any of them. Plus, none of them were paid positions. I needed to make money to get through the summer. I had to have this internship to graduate, and I wasn't quite ready to leave the East Coast. I was feeling better and getting out every weekend to explore. I had a New England travel guide. Every weekend I would leave to visit various parts of the East. I had not visited all the spots I wanted to. Mark and I were chatting again. We had decided we would give it another go—I would spend the summer living with him at his parents' house in Bolton, Massachusetts.

I got out a map and decided I was willing to drive up to 30 miles from Bolton for my internship. So I sent 22 letters with my resume to all the hospitals nearby. It was your basic letter;

I gave them credentials, school, etc. I heard back from three hospitals and ended up with two job offers. I took the paid position at Lowell Massachusetts General Hospital. I knew there were going to be conflicts with my Montana professor about being paid for my position. It was a six-credit internship and we were not supposed to be paid. I decided I would deal with the consequences when I got back to Montana. I was a high-achieving student, president of the Nutrition Club at MSU, and in the Nutrition Club at UConn. I also was in the Nutrition National Honor Society and president of the Montana State University chapter. In addition to that, I had worked in the Food Science Lab at MSU under the other nutrition professor. I was *not* concerned about six credits. I knew the experience would be amazing.

LESSON

Creativity

I think you need to creatively teach your children that they need to make a life that works for them. I want our children to follow the rules, but I also want our children to be creative. If there is another way for them to fulfill their goals or needs, then I want them to reach for that. One year Ian was supposed to carry three huge three-ring binders to and from school. His grade school was very good and strict about teaching students how to organize themselves and how to study. But Ian was really struggling to get his books to and from school; he walked both ways. I had him lay out all his work and show me his system for school. He and I came up with a new system to get his schoolwork to and from school. He ended up carrying very little home every night. The teacher never said a word, and Ian was very happy with his new system. I don't want our kids to be rule breakers, but I do want them to learn how to arrange their lives so their lives work for them.

After my summer internship, my boyfriend and I parted ways, and I drove back to Montana. (A side note that wasn't funny at the time, but is now: the day before I left Massachusetts I went for a run. I had to go to the bathroom and not number one. So like any smart runner, I used a few leaves as toilet paper. About ten hours into my drive back to Montana, I realized what I had used for toilet paper was poison oak. I had to stop at the emergency room in Pennsylvania for a cortisone shot. I finished the rest of my drive to Montana sitting on an ice pack.)

I wrapped up my senior year at Montana State University and drove back to Portland the day of my graduation. I skipped the graduation. I'd gone to Mark's two years before, and it was so boring; I didn't want to sit through mine. Plus, my parents said they weren't coming. I got back to Portland with no job and no interest in working in the nutrition world. My internship had burned me out; the doctors didn't really listen to the nutrition prescriptions we wrote. I knew that if I wanted to stay in the healthcare world I either needed to go to medical school or to figure out a new plan. While I contemplated my career, I took a job temping at Nike; a month later I got fired.

LESSON

Consequences

Do not bail your kids out. I'm talking about jail and any other trouble they get themselves into. Let your children live, breathe, and feel the consequences of their choices, both good and bad. Let them learn. If our kids forget to take their lunches to school, I don't bring their lunches for them. They have to deal. Harvey didn't take his lunch to school the other day. He just forgot it. I knew he forgot it; I saw it in the fridge as I was cleaning up the kitchen after breakfast. Harvey had already loaded himself in the car. So I left his lunch in the fridge and took everyone to school, including Harvey. Harvey was fine; the teacher gave him a few crackers. All of our children have forgotten their lunches. It generally happens about once a year for each child. If I bailed Harvey out and brought his lunch or reminded him to bring his lunch, how would he learn to remember his lunch? He wouldn't.

I want our children to manage their lives and their things, and to take responsibility for what is happening in their lives. I don't want to have a sixth-grade kid who calls to tell me he forgot his homework. I want that child to experience the consequences of forgetting his homework. I want those consequences to teach our children to remember their homework next time. The counselor I see from time to time tells me this is called consequential learning or natural consequences.

LESSON

Sticking to Your Words

A spin-off lesson from this is that I want to teach our kids to stick to their words. One morning we offered Ian tickets to the local soccer game. Whenever I offer the kids something, I give them a firm deadline to give me answer. I told Ian he needed to give me an answer by 10:00 a.m., after his Confirmation class. He came home at 10:00 a.m. and said he didn't want to go to the game. No biggie. David decided to take Harvey and Teddy. At about 2:00 p.m. (the game started at 4:00 p.m.), Ian decided he wanted to go to the game with Teddy and David because he was having so much fun hanging out with them. But we had already told Harvey he could go. David asked what to do. I thought it was sweet that Ian wanted to go, but we had already promised Harvey he could go. It wouldn't be right to take the ticket away from Harvey. Nor would it be right to purchase another ticket for Ian. Ian was upset, but he understood. If he went, Harvey wouldn't get to go, and purchasing another ticket was out of the question. This was a very simple situation, but it was a huge learning opportunity for Ian. No, I did not explain all the things Ian was learning in this situation; I just let experience do the teaching.

That same day, I was hopping in the car at 5:50 p.m. to pick the boys up from the game. Wiggy said she wanted to stay at home. So when it was time for me to leave, I said goodbye to Ian and Wiggy and got in the car. One minute later, Ian was running down the driveway to tell me Wiggy wanted to ride in the car. It's the same story: Wiggy had already decided to stay home. I want my kids to learn to make decisions and stick to them. I told Wiggy I was sorry but that she said she wanted to stay home, and that I would be home very soon. It was not a big deal whether Wiggy rode in the car with me or not. What was a big deal was teaching her to make decisions and understand the consequences. So, folks, don't let your kiddos be wishy-washy. If your child says she would like to play soccer, and if you are willing to stand in the rain for soccer, and if the practices and games fit with your family, then sign your child up for soccer. If your kiddo goes to the first practice and cries and says she doesn't want to play and on and on and on, it's going to be a long season, but your child will learn an important lesson. Once you commit to something, you stick with it. If you are at a restaurant and your son orders pizza, and when dinner comes, he decides he wants your dinner instead, the answer is no. You are happy to share a few bites, but you are not trading dinners with your child. You eat your meal and he eats his.

ANOTHER LESSON

Discipline with Manners

We do our best to discipline all of our children with manners. I tell my kids I'm sorry all the time. "I'm sorry you made that decision," "I'm sorry you don't want to go to bed," "I'm sorry you decided to hit your sister," "I'm sorry you decided to scream at the table." I am sorry our kids have made poor decisions, and I'm sorry I have to discipline a child. And when I say I'm sorry, I have a chance to pause, to calm down, and to collect my thoughts. Generally, I'm saying, "I'm sorry, have a seat on the stair" (more on what that means later). The point is for us parents to eliminate the screaming, the rude tones of voice, and the shaming, and to try to just get some simple disciplining done with a gentle voice, simple words, and manners.

After Nike, I quickly got my act together and found a job as a food sales representative. This was not a pretty job, but it mixed food (which I knew very well) with business (which I was very interested in). The job entailed me selling food to restaurants, schools, hospitals, and any other place I could find. The food business was busy, but lonely. I worked out of my house, solo. I went out a lot. On one of those nights I was out partying, I ran into a friend who worked at Enron, and she mentioned she was leaving her job and that I should apply. So on my way to Sun Valley for a vacation, I stopped in at Enron for a job interview. I started at Enron two weeks later. And I ended at Enron about eight months later with everyone else.

Enron was wild. I worked on the trading floor when megawatts were priced over $1,000. My job was to enter trades for the traders and balance their books. The trading floor was so fun. There was music, footballs flying, TVs everywhere, swearing, chewing tobacco (something I have enjoyed since age 14), great people, free breakfast if you got there early, and constant partying. Trading looked fun, and I wanted to try it. I told my boss I wanted to trade. He said "no." I kept asking until he said "yes." He said to show up at 4:15 a.m. I showed up and occasionally I was given a few odd-lot megawatts to trade. I continued to show up and continued to trade odd lots. But when everything started to crumble at Enron, like everyone else I was let go.

LESSON

Really Going For It

I'll say it again. Teach your children to GO FOR IT! Teach your children to go after their lives, after their dreams, after their loves, after everything. I wanted to trade; I had a nutrition degree. Enron was filled with an amazing group of educated folks. I didn't let my nutrition degree slow me down or get in my way for a second. I didn't think about my degree because I knew it would have slowed me down; most people at Enron were Ivy League educated. I just forged ahead to get where I wanted.

Before Enron fell apart, I had been asked to be the assistant coach for my high school ski team. It was good timing because I was about to need the extra income, and the season ski pass was an added bonus. Being let go from Enron was the fourth job I had lost. The first two were in Sun Valley; one was for swearing on a painting job and the other was for showing up to Smoky Mountain Pizza stoned. (I didn't get fired for being stoned (my boss didn't know that). I got fired because I walked in the back door, saw how busy we were, and walked back home. I was too stoned to deal. I can't believe pot is legal.) The third job was Nike, and then Enron.

Anyway, I was let go from Enron like thousands of others. Thankfully, I only had myself to support; my rent was manageable on unemployment. I searched and searched for a job. But the entire country was collapsing. Finally ... I landed a job with a family friend doing marketing for an osteoporosis research company, Oregon Osteoporosis Research. My job was to recruit candidates for pharmaceutical studies. I had learned enough about the body and how it works from my nutrition degree to discuss the research process with potential candidates. The rest I had to learn. I had never written a radio advertisement, placed an advertisement in the paper, sent out mass mailings, or purchased mailing lists; it was all new. My boss was very supportive of me taking classes. If I needed to learn something, I would find a class, present him with my idea, and then go take the class. It really was an amazing experience. I had the research office busier than it had ever been. I was a little recruiting machine.

LESSON

Qualifications

This goes for kids and adults. Don't ever not go for something because you think you aren't qualified. Ever. I didn't think I was qualified for the research job or to trade at Enron. I wanted those jobs. Teach your children and yourself to go for everything. And don't quit until you get it. Remember my Enron boss? I just kept asking until he said "yes." I have always thought of "no" as a jumping-off point. It's a jumping-off point because it's hard to ask for what you want the first time—but the second time is easier and the third time is a breeze. You just need to find a different angle or work a little harder. There is always a way.

After Enron I started making jewelry. The basic stuff: putting beads on strings. You can't look for a job ten hours a day, so I found a hobby—a passion, if you will. It was really fun, but very expensive for someone with no income. My friends were asking me to make them stuff, but I couldn't afford to unless I charged them. I decided to have a jewelry party. I sold everything and made a nice little bundle of cash. I made a few more pieces and went around town selling my wares. I had four retail clients in Portland and Eugene. My grandfather's father-in-law started the company Norm Thompson; our family no longer owned the business, but we still had connections, so I went to their offices and pitched my jewelry to them. Boom: I sold 2,000 necklaces in one meeting. Yes, that meant I had to make 2,000 necklaces. But I was only working 40 hours a week at my research job and coaching skiing a little bit. I was young, with tons of energy. Typically, I would go to my research job around 8:00 a.m., work until 4:00 p.m., head to the gym or go for a run, and then work on jewelry until 1:00 or 2:00 a.m. On Wednesday nights and Saturday mornings, I would coach skiing. I was busy—very busy—but I loved it.

The great thing about my research job was that I made my own hours. So the 8:00 a.m. to 4:00 p.m. typical hours were not mandatory. I could easily squeeze in a jewelry show or meeting and then work a few extra hours in the evening or during the weekend. Jewelry became very successful; my second year of making jewelry, my income skyrocketed to $110,000—that was on top of what I earned with my research job and skiing. I was doing fine. I was considering quitting the research job to do jewelry full-time. And just as I was penciling out insurance and office space, an old co-worker from Enron called and asked if I would like to interview as a trading assistant at PacifiCorp. Remember, I had worked solo before and did not like it; the jewelry business would be like that, for a while anyway. In addition, jewelry styles were changing and beading was becoming less fashionable, and I knew it. Metalsmithing was the next step, but I had taken a few classes and wasn't as inspired by it. So I closed up my jewelry shop and took a job with PacifiCorp. It was so fun to be back on the floor. I loved it! And then eight months later, another co-worker from Enron called and asked if I wanted to interview for a trading position at PPM Energy. The job I had wanted and worked towards since my Enron days was being dangled in front of me.

I got the trading job at PPM Energy (now Iberdrola). I was on cloud nine. I really felt like I had succeeded in so many areas of my life. And my boys' ski team had just won their state competition as I was coaching my final year and accepting my trading position. Life was pretty good. I walked into my first day at PPM, and there were all my old Enron buddies, as well as some new faces. I was the only female trader; it was me and the guys. I had a lot to learn—I mean a lot. My head was pretty big from growing a successful jewelry company and then landing a job as a commodities trader with a nutrition degree. But my new job quickly brought me out of the clouds. I had so much to learn, and I remembered nothing from my Enron days. Being back with the Enron crew meant long nights of partying and early mornings or night shifts. Thankfully, I had the stamina; instead of three jobs, I only had one.

LESSON

Work

Teach your children to work. Teach your children early to work. Our kids all work around our home, and I call it work. Sure, sometimes work sucks, but for the most part, if you find something you love, you can do it for hours on end. I used to be able to stay up for hours plugging away on jewelry. At PPM we had so much fun at work you wouldn't realize you were 10 hours into a 12-hour shift. When I was 10 years old and we moved into our rental house, I learned how to work from helping my mom around the house and completing what I started. I learned to work hard from the sports I played. This was back in the day when you just dealt with a shitty coach. I had ski coaches who grabbed our asses and snorted cocaine. We never said anything; we just worked hard and skied. I'm not saying their behavior was right—it wasn't. But we were there to ski. Your children are not always going to have great teachers or coaches, and you aren't always going to be the perfect parent, but teach your children to navigate the shitty waters of life. Don't be the parent that bitches because you aren't happy with your child's coaches, teachers, or peers. Teach your child how to speak up for himself or accept his situation. Now, I don't want you to stick with the teachers or coaches that are inappropriate or don't lift a finger. But if it really isn't that bad for your child, let it go. Ian has a teacher that isn't great right now. We talk about the teacher, and instead of getting on Ian's level and complaining with him, we talk about ways to possibly make it better. Your children are going to have future bosses who aren't great; teach your children how to deal with those folks now.

I got off the point. The point of this lesson is to teach your children to work. My kids work around the house, and a lot. I do not make lunches, put away laundry, clean bedrooms, or make anyone's bed but my own. Our children do all of this for themselves. If our kids don't feel like making their lunch for school, my reply is very simple: "That's your choice." If my kids don't make their beds, I charge them money. Yep: cold cash. Our children can pull their weight. They are capable and able. I am not a maid, assistant, or housekeeper. I am a mother; my job is to love our children and raise them. A big part of that is having them manage as much of their lives as they can.

I'll point out real quick, I do my best not to yell at, nag, or shame our children if they haven't done what I want, or if they have done something wrong. Instead, I try to take one of two approaches. One, I am a broken record. "I'm sorry you don't want to take a shower, let me help you take your shirt off. I'm sorry you don't want to take a shower . . ." And so on. Ninety-five percent of the time, while our kids are arguing about doing whatever we are asking, they are on their way to do it anyway. So I just politely keep the conversation going. Or I handle things by saying nothing. If I have a kid getting ready slowly in the morning, I don't say a word. I let him learn—when he comes downstairs and we are all loading in the car—that he misses breakfast. It's sad to see your child upset because he missed a meal, but it's so great the next morning when you see that kiddo hustling to make it to breakfast. These are natural consequences, and you don't need to get involved. The situation will teach your child all he needs to learn. Don't get me wrong: there are those times when you just want to yell and scream at your children. It happens, folks. I lose my cool from time to time; it just happens. Sometimes you have just had it.

I had been trading at PPM for five years. It was time for me to move up. I was one of the lead traders on my desk. I needed to move on. So I applied to trade and manage our 506 megawatt gas-fired plant. I would still be trading in our Portland office. I got the job and quickly realized it wasn't what I wanted to do. I didn't like the daily trading market. I liked the quick pace of the hourly market. I did the job well, but I knew deep down I needed to find something else. A year later, I was approached about a mid-marketing job. I would meet with customers all over the West Coast (and eventually, the East Coast), working to set up longer-term deals ... multimillion-dollar deals. Again, I got the job.

Oops, I almost forgot. A couple of years before this, I met David, the fella I am married to now. David and I met at a lunch. I was having an informational interview with one of David's previous partners at a local consulting firm. I was doing great at my job, but I was curious what other opportunities were out there. Within five minutes of the start of the lunch meeting, they both (almost in unison) told me I was not the caliber of employee they were looking for. We had not even ordered lunch. I was like, OMG, how do we salvage this lunch! Should I just get up and walk out? I had just returned from Thailand, so I quickly changed the subject to my trip. David had just gotten back from a trip to Peru with his sister, and I was thinking about taking my brother to Peru. We had a topic and I didn't have to do the talking. So David and I talked and talked (he likes to talk; we are working on his listening skills all the time) and he swore a lot too. And then I realized, except for his choice in shoes, he had good style, and I liked his hair (brown at the time). He was kinda hot. At the end of the lunch, he gave me his business card and said if I wanted to know more about Peru to give him a call. Sure I wanted to know more Peru, but I also wanted to know more about this hot guy. So I called him up. He answered the phone (as he still does), "This is David."

"Hi, David. It's Kysa."

"Who?"

WTF? "Kysa. We had lunch the other day. I was wondering if we could get together and talk about Peru."

"Ah, sure. I'm pretty busy. When?"

Jeez! This guy isn't interested or he's a complete jerk. Or he has a girlfriend, because he didn't have a ring. I said, "Friday."

"Sure, fine. Where?"

Swallowing my pride. "The Goose Hollow."

"Fine." And he hung up.

Our first date was amazing. We were supposed to meet at the bar, but I started the evening a little early, playing football and drinking beers at a park with the guys from work. I missed our meeting time at the bar, so we ended up meeting at a local grocery store to grab a six-pack and head to a park to let our dogs run. We ended the night with dinner at a yummy Peruvian restaurant and a steamy kiss in the grocery store parking lot. For the most part, we have been tied at the hip ever since.

When David and I weren't working, we were up partying all night, sleeping in, and doing fun stuff during the day. I would have never thought I was fertile, but I am very fertile. David and I never used protection, and in the beginning of dating, we were like rabbits on steroids. One afternoon before working the night shift, I was working out at the gym, and towards the end of my workout, I felt pressure. So I wrapped up my workout and got in the shower, where I discovered I was bleeding. I felt down and out came two pink kidney-shaped forms. I thought they might be babies, but I didn't know I was pregnant. I wrapped them up and tucked them in my bag. I was in shock. Imagine something falling out of your body with blood.

David and I weren't dating at the time—he was very wishy-washy at the beginning of our relationship. Get married to me? Not get married to me? So many times I got so fed up with David and his indecision that I would tell him to pound sand. I would absolutely love to dish more on this portion of my life, but it isn't just my story, and I cannot and will not share. That evening around midnight, I was able to step away from the trading desk and phone the on-call doctor. I had miscarried twins. I accepted the news from the doctor and went back to working. Was I sad? Yes. But I was more in shock. I had always thought with all my reckless behavior that my body couldn't bear children. Turns out I was wrong. Later, I told David about my miscarriage.

Back to my career. David and I were buzzing along. I obviously did not get a job with the consulting company; instead, I got one of the owners. I took the mid-market job at Iberdrola. David proposed, and I sold my house (I had purchased a house two years and two days before) and moved in with him. David had hip replacement surgery, and then David and I bought a new house, and I found out I was pregnant. That was a stressful time; it's a blur. I had already been spending time with David and Ian, so living with them wasn't really a big change. Now it was the three of us and our four dogs under one roof. I had been a stepdaughter, and my experience was not good. I knew I would never take over for or compare to Ian's mom. But I knew I could try my best to be a positive figure in his life. There were things with Ian I had to change right away. I insisted Ian have a bedtime every night, make his bed every morning, and clean up after himself. I insisted we sit down at the dining room table for dinner together. With the exception of our family dinners, all of this drove David crazy in the beginning, because Ian was pissed about the changes. But what kid wouldn't be pissed?

We worked through all the new rules, and I learned very quickly that consistency is the key to healthy, happy kids. If you are consistent with your children, they will always know where they stand and what is expected of them. I also learned to pay close attention as I was rolling out the new rules. With regard to bedtime, neither David nor Ian was a huge fan. So I would start preparing them 30 minutes before Ian actually had to be in bed. Ian hemmed and hawed and begged to stay up. If I wasn't standing nearby, Ian would get to stay up past the 7:00 bedtime. Over time, Ian and David realized I wasn't budging on the bedtime, so they gave up fighting. I was also very gentle as I made these changes. I always spoke in a calm voice, telling them it was dinnertime or time for bed. And over time we were humming right along.

LESSON

Consistency

If you would like to have rules in your house, first make sure you and your partner and anyone else who helps you with your family are willing and able to carry out your rules with consistency, kindness, and love. David and I were not on the same page in the beginning. I was solo, but I knew my changes were good for all of us. I was parenting Ian and teaching David to parent. Like I said, it was slow, but we got there. I do not say this lightly. Set rules that you, the parent, the leader, the commander of your home, can stick with and teach the other caretakers in your family. There is absolutely no point in making a rule for you or your children that you know you cannot stick to.

If the bedtime in your home is 7:00 p.m., that does not mean 7:05 p.m. If you can't stick to 7:00 p.m., then give your children a bedtime you can stick to. I learned with Ian that if he was allowed to stay up 30 minutes, we had a battle for the following three nights about his bedtime. But if we just stuck to his bedtime of 7:00 p.m., it became routine, and he also knew that we were not budging, so he wouldn't waste his time arguing. If you can't keep the 7:30 p.m. bedtime, start baths/showers earlier, or get help. Call your aunt, mother, friend, or neighbor to show up every night to help you get the process going. Sometimes you have to be extreme. It took me two years to streamline our bedtime routine. I used to have to head upstairs at 5:30 p.m. to get the kids bathed, read to, and in bed by 7:00 p.m. Now we can do it in 30 minutes. It took a lot of patience, consistency, and training—for both myself and our children.

The goal was for the kids to learn the routine and for me to keep the program consistent.

In our house our children shower every night. We read books every night (well almost every night). And lights are out and doors are closed at 7:00 p.m. No one can question anything, because we don't add a lot of excitement to a very challenging time of day. We keep it very consistent and very simple. I highly recommend keeping the sensitive times in your home consistent. Sensitive times in our house are bedtime and getting ready for school. The kids know what is expected of them. We have never gotten in bed with our children to snuggle them to sleep; our children do not crawl into our bed in the middle of night. We have never allowed these activities, so we don't have any bad bedtime routines to break. And that is the key point. Do not start difficult behaviors or habits with your children and you will not have to help them unlearn them. So check in with yourself whenever you are doing a new activity with your kids ... ask yourself if you can keep this up every day or evening. If the answer is no, then you must tell your child the same thing.

Let me give you an example. Your child wants to start brushing her teeth in the bathtub or shower. Fast forward two weeks and see if you can continue doing this each night. If you can, great; give your child the green light. We do this, and it's great. Now consider this example: your child would like to begin the night sleeping in your bed, and when she falls asleep, she would like you to carry her to her bed. Again, fast forward two weeks or two months. Would you like to do this every night? No? Me neither. The answer would be, "No, I'm sorry, that's not an option. Now, let's tuck you in real cozy to your bed." And one more example so you can see what I am getting at: your little ones would like to put their pajamas on by the front door in anticipation of their father coming home from a business trip. That might be fine this time, but what about the time when his flight is delayed or his flight lands at 11:00 p.m.? It's not a good program. Yes, your little ones might be bummed when you say no, but this is not a life changer, folks. At this time of night, the family job is to get the children to bed so they can get all the sleep they need. So, again, the answer is, "No, I'm sorry. Let's get you tucked in and we will see Daddy in the morning for breakfast."

I was pregnant with Teddy, the new house was great, Ian was doing great, my job was great, I was traveling a lot, David and I got married, and then a bomb was dropped. I found out my mom had cancer. It's true that in an instant life can change, and mine did. I was a stepmom, pregnant, traveling for my new job, taking care of my sick mom, and trying to navigate the first year of marriage. Life for David and me started at a fast pace, and it hasn't slowed down since.

I would get up in the morning, swing by my mom's condo to check on her, head to work, leave work at lunch to check on my mom, and go back to work. After work I would check on my mom, and then hopefully go home to sleep after I had made dinner and fed the dogs. I would pray at night that my mom wouldn't call because she needed something; all I wanted to do was sleep. I know that sounds horrible, but I was so tired trying to manage everything and growing a baby in my belly.

There was other drama too. My mom was struggling finan-cially. I knew she had always had a little trouble with money. She owed a lot of money on the condo she owned. David and I had to foreclose on her condo and find her a new place to live on a very tight budget and following a very long and stressful surgery to remove the majority of her cancer. A month after my mom's surgery, we were handing over her apartment keys to the bank and wheeling her stuff into a rental.

It all happened so fast. I can't even describe how crazy it was. And the whole time, everyone was telling me all this stress was bad for the baby in my belly. I couldn't just leave my mom high and dry; and I couldn't just leave my job. I had to do what I had to do. I had to start putting myself first. I had to pull from those great lessons I had taught myself in college, during my days of depression.

LESSON

Making Time for Yourself

Guess who comes first in my house? Me. Yes, I cook what I want for dinner. If I want to exercise, I find time and go do it. If I need to shower, I just lay a baby on the floor next to the shower and take a shower. If I want to go for a hike, I organize our life so we can go for a hike. If I need time with friends, I do it. I am always surprised when I hear someone say "I haven't taken a shower in days because of the kids." Really? Pull your children into the bathroom, shut the door, and take a shower. I know it's hard to find time to do things with children, but figure it out and do it. The happier I am, the calmer, saner, and kinder I am as a mother. And the calmer, saner, and kinder my entire family is. I am friends with those moms who are killing themselves to be perfect moms. I am not that mom, and I am not capable of being that mom. You will not see me killing myself to bake the perfect birthday cake; I buy cakes. You will not see me stressing out to produce the perfect playdate for one of our kids; it is their job to have successful playdate. (Of course, playdates may need assistance from time to time. More on that later.) You will not see me running all over town to purchase school supplies; I will have kids in tow for some quality time, and our children can be involved in the process. I am not a hero mom—no way; I don't have the energy for it. And I do not in the slightest bit think hero moms make, produce, or create better children. I think hero moms are exhausted—but more power to them.

I think our children are better people because I am not a hero mom, bending over backwards to make their lives easier and simpler. I learned during that time with my mom that to keep my sanity I had to put my needs first. Now that I have kids, it is no different. I still put myself first. Yes, I have had to find some creative ways to get my needs met before I meet the needs of our children. To do this, I get up at 4:00 a.m. to do dishes, laundry, email, and most importantly, enjoy my wonderful cup of Folgers crystals with a tiny bit of whole milk and tiny bit of hazelnut creamer ... delicious. At 5:00 a.m. I am exercising, and by 6:30 a.m. I am showered and ready for our children. Moms, dads, caregivers: put yourself first. Your children will be better humans for it. They also will learn to start meeting their own needs rather than always counting on someone else to meet their needs for them.

On May 8, a week past my due date, I went into the hospital to have a pregnancy stress test. I was kept in the hospital due to my amniotic fluid level (which was almost zero) and started on a uterine stimulant to start contractions. After twelve hours of the medication, there were no changes in my cervix. The doctor came in and said I could do another twelve-hour round of Pitocin or have a C-section and meet my baby in 30 minutes. I chose instant gratification and opted for a C-section. I hated it. The drugs make you feel horrible. But … it took 30 minutes and we got to meet our baby boy, Theodore (Teddy) Alport Kelleher. Let the nursing, napping, and baby games begin.

Now I was a stepmom *and* a mom. Because I was so busy moving into our house, taking care of myself, digesting the first year of marriage, accepting my new role as a stepmom, and taking care of my dying mother, I hadn't really thought much about bringing an infant into the mix. I also did not read any books on motherhood or pregnancy before Teddy was born. I was just too busy or too tired.

My mom was not getting better. But I was happy to give her a grandson. It was another difficult time. I wasn't in much shape to take care of my mom with a newborn, a stepson, and my C-section. My mom and I fought and then got along and then fought again. Back in January, she had written me out of her will. She didn't know I knew she did this. I was so hurt by her actions, but my mom was so sick that I didn't confront her. After Teddy was born, it didn't really matter; I had bigger things to focus on. I felt the difference between having my own child and having a stepson. There was a huge difference for me. I did not love Ian the same way I loved Teddy, but I loved Ian dearly. So from May to August, I was searching my heart and trying to figure out how to navigate my new feelings about motherhood while watching my mother die. I tried to open up to David about my troubled feelings about Ian, and he was so disappointed. But I felt the way I felt. It wasn't Ian; he had nothing to do with it. It was just life. I had carried Teddy in my belly and I hadn't carried Ian. I could not argue with my feelings, they were so real.

I remember it so vividly: the gate would slam shut as Ian walked in from school. I would just freeze. I would plaster a smile on my face the minute he walked in the door. Again, it had nothing to do with Ian; it had to do with being the same mother to my son and my stepson. I needed a plan because I was in very murky waters. I had no one to turn to. I know from being a stepchild myself that it's rough. I was never, ever treated the same as my half-brother was treated, and it burned deep every time. So with Ian I decided that every time I snuggled Teddy or offered him food or anything, I would do the same for Ian. Over time, my plan worked. Today David understands what I felt back then. And today I feel the same about Ian as I do about my other children. I love them *all* so much.

I don't really remember what kind of monster I was with all that was happening; I am sure I was horrible. David stood by me like the soldier he is. He helped me with my mom. My mom would call David out of meetings to bring her lunch or change her post-surgery bandages. She loved David! Every day was a rodeo. It was scary, it was financially straining, it was embarrassing to ask my new husband to help me with my messy family, it was exhausting. Through it all, I learned to be consistent in taking care of myself. I never knew what the day would throw at me. Would I be calling an ambulance to get my mom to the hospital? Would a doctor be calling to tell me my mom's numbers were bad? Would Teddy just cry the entire day? I never knew. But I knew if I got up, exercised, and got the house in order, I could check that off my list. And to this day, I can handle pretty much *anything* if I get up and have both of those things in order.

LESSON

Taking Care of Yourself

Teach yourself to take care of yourself. Carve the time out of your day to feed your soul and take care of your body. I'm not saying bust your booty to fit into size-two jeans. I'm saying bust it to figure out what makes your days go smoothly and figure out a way to do it. For me, I like to get up early, make my coffee, empty the dishwasher, tidy up the house, fold the laundry, check my email, and take a look at our family schedule for the day. Some mornings I leave the dishwasher filled and the laundry unfolded and read a magazine while I sip my coffee. The goal for me is to have the morning to myself.

So figure out what makes you tick or not tick. And, yes, all of my friends think I am out of my mind for getting up before the crack of dawn, 4:00 a.m. But it works for me.

ANOTHER LESSON

Accepting Help

During my period of being a new mom and stepmom and watching my mom die, I needed all the help I could get. I didn't have a choice. I hated taking Teddy into the hospital to see my mom—I truly hated it. It wasn't that I didn't want to spend time with Teddy or my mom. I didn't want my newborn to be exposed to all the diseases in the hospital. But I was nursing, so he and I were always together. If anyone visiting my mom offered to walk him around the block or watch him so I could care for my mom, I never said no.

If you are at a place in your life when you need help—because of marriage troubles, a new baby, sickness, carpooling, whatever it is—take all the help you can get. If someone offers to help you out with anything—childcare, picking up diapers at Costco, cooking you dinner, whatever—just take it. It's hard to accept help, but I think it's even harder to ask for help. So if you allow someone to help you out, you will be doing them a favor, because you have opened the door. When your friends need help, they will be more inclined to ask you for help the next time they are in need. So always accept help when someone offers. You deserve it. And always offer help when you see someone in need.

My mom was not doing well; we couldn't get her to eat. We fed her with a tube through her nose for a while, but she absolutely hated it. We couldn't get her pain meds correct. I spoke to a pain specialist and tried to educate myself on pain management over the phone. Out of the blue, my mom got very sick; she wasn't eating or using the bathroom, and she couldn't get out of bed. We took her to the hospital and they ran a lot of tests. I had left the hospital to take our four dogs (two labs and two terriers) to the vet, with Teddy in tow. I was trying to get the dogs out of the car on a busy road a block from the vet, hold onto the leashes, and get Teddy's car seat in the Snap-N-Go. I was expecting a call from the doc, and it came as I really had my hands full. So I stood on the side of the road with all the dogs barking, Teddy sleeping, listening to the doctor tell me that my mom had taken something that had shut down her liver. He wasn't sure if she would make it through the night. I needed to go to her condo and figure out what she had taken. So I loaded the dogs and Teddy back up and drove to her condo. All I could find were some herbs and Tylenol. I called the doc, explained what I had found, and he gave her a medication to hopefully reverse the effects of the massive doses of Tylenol we assumed she had taken. The "reversal" medication would take 24 hours before we would know if it worked. That was a long 24 hours of my mom lying in bed, looking like she had already died. Finally, she started to come to; the medication worked. My mom recovered from the Tylenol. Later, my mom told me she tried to manage her pain with Tylenol instead of her prescribed pain medications.

My mom had to stay in the hospital for a week to improve her eating and get hydrated. She hated the hospital, but I loved it. I knew my mom was safe. My phone was less likely to ring during the day or in the middle of the night with an emergency. We had looked into a full-time nurse, but I couldn't afford it after quitting my job (more on my job soon). And my mom certainly couldn't afford it. We had talked about me moving in to take care of her, but I was still nursing Teddy in the middle of the night. And my mom lived in a studio. Plus, I really wanted to curl up with the calm safeness of David every night. On the other hand, my mom didn't want to move in with us. It was a mess. I felt like such a brat for not packing up Teddy and moving into my mom's. But I would still have to be at my house so much because I still had Ian half the time and the dogs to take care of. So I would have been all over the place. I just couldn't do it all.

On top of that, nursing was brutal. In the beginning, I struggled to get Teddy to latch on. After Teddy was born, I had the lactation nurse in my hospital room for every feeding. Then when I could latch Teddy on myself, I screamed because it hurt so badly. I almost punched a hole in the wall one time. It was awful. But I learned in school how good it was for the baby and how cost effective it was. And a girl I worked with long ago told me to hang on through the pain for six weeks. After six weeks the pain would go away and it would be a breeze. She was so right. After six weeks, nursing was a breeze. And one thing no one ever tells you about nursing: it's a guaranteed 15 to 30 minutes of quiet, relaxing time off your feet every three hours. New moms *need* this.

Sadly, on August 2, my mom passed away from complications associated with her cancer.

Teddy was born on May 9, and my maternity leave was up seven days after my mom passed. I had to go back to work. We had tried to find a daycare, but I was so uninterested in looking into daycares during the last month of my mom's life. So I went back to work and, temporarily, David stayed home with Teddy. It was good to see everyone at work, but when I sat down to read my email, I was so confused. I couldn't understand what I was reading. I couldn't focus. I was so tired and sad. I got to work at 7:00 a.m. my first day back and left at about 10:00 a.m. I couldn't handle it, or I didn't want to. I didn't want to be at work. I wanted to be home on our couch sleeping and taking care of Teddy and our house. That night I called my boss at

9:00 p.m. and quit my beloved job. I was happy I would not have to find childcare, happy I didn't have to rush Ian and Teddy around so I could get to work, and happy I could relax and let the past year sink into the past. But I was also very sad to leave a career that was ten years in the making. I love being a mom, but I do miss my career. I worked so hard to get there.

When I went downstairs that night to tell David I had quit my job, he was a little shocked. He said we were probably going to have to move from our new house. I was okay with all of that. I knew I could not mentally handle all that had happened; I had to let something go. Without notice, I became a stay-at-home mom. And, without notice, David became our primary breadwinner.

Back to nursing. In the hospital, the nurse told me to feed Teddy every three hours. She said try to avoid "on-demand" feeding. So I set the timer on my watch to 3:00 hours. When the timer went off, I fed Teddy.

LESSON

Scheduling

I knew I wasn't going to parent "on-demand" so I wasn't going to start Teddy's life that way. He was going to eat on my schedule. They say never wake a sleeping baby. I never understood that. Babies easily fall back asleep, so might as well wake 'em up, feed 'em, and let them teach themselves to fall back asleep. Plus, my little timer allowed me to really get to know Teddy. If he was upset, it was either because he was tired or needed his diaper changed. And I didn't turn him into an emotional eater. Think about all these babies who get a bottle or boob shoved in their mouth to stop their crying ... won't that cause emotional eating? It certainly will cause some need to orally fixate themselves when they are upset. Anyway, with my little stopwatch system, I was able to check my watch and see that I had two hours to grocery shop, fold laundry, work out, run soccer carpool, or whatever until my next feeding. For me, scheduling worked very well. Sure, at times it was a drag to keep the nap schedule or feeding schedule, but it always made for a happier and well-rested baby.

ANOTHER LESSON

Sleep

Sleep deprivation is a form of torture. So make sure sleeping is a priority for you and for your newborn and any other member of your family. Get a sleep program in your home and stick with it. Do not wing this job. Do not roll with the punches of your baby. Do not let your baby decide. Give yourself sleep, sanity, and a life. Put your babies and children down for naps. Talk with your friends and doctors and read books and figure out what system will work for you, your baby, your family, and then stick with it. I let my babies cry it out. I didn't read all the studies about why children shouldn't cry it out. I figured babies needed sleep; I needed sleep so we were going to nail this little program down. No joke, sleep-training is difficult for everyone. But sleep is so important, and I wanted to teach our children to teach themselves to fall asleep. David and I stuck to our guns. We have had the same sleep hours we did when Teddy was six months old, 7:00 p.m. to 7:00 a.m. Our children all have alarms in their rooms and they are not allowed to get out of their beds until their alarms tell them so in the morning. They each have a stack of books to read or look at by their beds until it's time to get up.

Now let's give some major credit where credit is due. David did all the sleep-training when we were given the green light by our family physician to let the babies sleep six hours, then ten hours, then twelve hours without feeding. David faithfully managed all of this. He kept me calm and turned down the baby monitor while each of our babies cried themselves to sleep.

We also have kept our children in cribs until they were four years old and they could fully understand the bedtime routine. Yes, this means our children have remained in diapers overnight, but that little hardship has allowed David and me to sleep every night. I have known a lot of folks pregnant with their second child and not wanting to buy a second crib, so they move their two-year-olds or younger to big beds. Not us. We spent the extra $89 at IKEA and bought an extra crib. And the Kellehers are all sleeping through the night, every night, without any children running about or crawling in our bed. Buy or borrow the second crib, folks.

When Teddy was six months old, I fed him his first bite of food, which meant I missed a nursing, which meant I got my first period. I counted eleven days—bada-bing, bada-boom—

and nine months later, we had Wiggy (Murphy). So there I was with a newborn, a sixteen-month-old, and a nine-year-old.

At sixteen months, Teddy was not meeting one major milestone. He was not crawling or walking; he was scooting. For the most part, I was okay with it; I had heard horror stories of mothers nursing newborns while their walking toddler was nowhere to be found. All I had to do was shut the door and I could happily nurse Wiggy and know that Teddy couldn't go anywhere because he couldn't stand up and open doors. So in my mind, I was happy he didn't walk, but friends and family and even strangers were more than happy to give information and email articles and unsolicited advice about why Teddy didn't walk or crawl. And if Teddy didn't crawl that he would have all sorts of learning disabilities because his right and left brain did not have the opportunity to make the connections crawling afforded the brain to make. I also had people tell me he didn't walk because I carried him everywhere. But I had to carry him because he didn't walk! I bought him at least two pairs of shorts or pants a week because of how quickly he would wear through the butt from scooting. It was tough and it was scary listening to what everyone said. I know nothing about the brain except that it sits on my neck. So most of the information people so kindly handed out freaked me the fuck out! But you can't make a kid walk.

LESSON

Opinions

People should zip it about other people's kids unless they are medically qualified to discuss such issues or their opinion is asked for. I was stressed out ... again. In less than two years, I got married, became a stepmom, lost my mom, and quit my job, and I had three children to care for. And when you are in that vulnerable spot where you don't really trust yourself, the last thing you need is some idiot's opinion. So if you have an issue with one of your children, find people who will support you and not give you ridiculous articles about what the future may look like for your family. Or if you don't want to hear what everyone has to say, then keep the on-goings in your life to yourself. I wish I had done that.

Keep your opinions to yourself unless you are asked for them. I am horrible at it! I really am, but I am trying all the time to be better. I am pregnant right now (more on that later), but cannot believe the stupid stuff people have said to me over the years.

I learned a lot during that time of Teddy not walking. I learned to have patience as a mother. I learned to do what worked for our family, and I started the learning process of ignoring others' comments and opinions. Our family pediatrician wanted me to take Teddy to physical therapy to learn to walk. So I packed up Wiggy and Teddy and away we went. It was awful. The therapist told me Teddy didn't walk because moms like me didn't put their babies on their bellies for tummy time, because they didn't want to hear their babies cry. She was right; I didn't want to hear my baby cry. I didn't want to listen to Teddy cry because Murphy was probably crying, or I was probably crying about my mom dying or my new role as a stepmom. I never went back to physical therapy. Teddy was the happiest little baby and his scooting around was adorable. His situation was *not* life threatening. So we decided to just let it go and see what happens.

Guess who's walking now? And guess who is reading now?

LESSON

What Works for Your Family

Sometimes the doctor's recommendations won't always work for your family. They may have a valid point or idea, but if it doesn't work for your family and you are happy and healthy the way you are, then stick to what you are doing. As you raise your kids, obtain and gain as much confidence in what you are doing at home. "The proof is in the pudding." If your family is running like a top and your kids are happy, stick with what you are doing. Teddy was absolutely happy the way he was. I didn't want my toddler to do two hours of therapy a day, and I didn't want to do two hours of therapy a day with my toddler. My sanity was far more important than forcing Teddy to walk.

You know your children and your spouse. You know deep down what works and what doesn't. Listen to that smart voice inside of you and do what works for you. Of course, if something in your family is not working, then find a way to fix it. Go ask other people for their opinions.

We were plugging along. I was getting the hang of three kids. Nursing Wiggy only hurt for a week, and it wasn't bad. I was managing cooking dinner, soccer carpool, a nursing schedule, napping, laundry, cleaning, and bedtime. Then David left for Germany with Ian. It was awful. I was exhausted. I was pissed off. I could not deal. I had no help, which was my own fault. It was me and two kids solo for ten days; I was a mess. A friend came over while David was gone and I was bitching to her. She said, "Are you pregnant?" It had not even dawned on me. Our sex life had taken a turn in another direction, barely existing. I had one "stick" left from testing for my pregnancy with Wiggy. Sure enough, smiley face. I was pregnant with Harvey. David called from Germany to get his daily bitch-out from home. This time I screamed on the phone at him about his trip; why couldn't he come home? At the end of the conversation, I screamed, "I'm pregnant!" and hung up. Oh what a lovely wife I can be ...

Teddy was two, and had finally started to put one foot in front of the other. He was walking! Wiggy was six months old. I got my period, counted eleven days, and—bada-bing, bada-boom—I was pregnant. I'm such a bitch when I'm pregnant. And the bitchiness doesn't stop after delivery; I continue on until our babies are two.

We had instantly grown out of our three-bedroom house. After Wiggy, I wanted to find a bigger house. We had Wiggy sleeping in the basement. I know, I know—I have heard it. But she was on a monitor so we could hear her, and our basement was finished. Wiggy took a long time to get on the sleep train, so she had to do her time far away. When David got back from Germany, he finally agreed that our three-bedroom house was not going to work for the six of us. We found a house four blocks away, similar to our current home, but with more bedrooms.

With Teddy and Wiggy, I had zero amniotic fluid left when they were born. So on one of the final visits to the doctor for Harvey, I asked them to check my fluid. The doctor said no, I begged and said I wasn't leaving until he checked. Sure enough, I had no amniotic fluid left. I was put on bed rest that day (Thursday) with the hope of making it to Monday. That same day, we got the keys to our new house, and the movers were coming the next morning at 6:00 a.m. Thankfully, I had labeled all the boxes and had printed out signs for all the rooms in the new house. All the boxes had a designated spot. In addition to that, I had found places for all four of our dogs to stay and places for three of our kids to stay. I was totally prepared for everything, except bed rest.

We called David's parents from the doctor's office, and they were on a flight that day from Atlanta, to lend us a hand. I don't know what we would have done without them. David's dad probably went to Home Depot 20 times and Fred Meyer 50 times during their two-week visit. We had nothing for the baby. Our car seat from Teddy and Wiggy was a hand-me-down, and we had given it back. Teddy's clothes were all trashed when he was done with them. We don't like to get anything before we have our babies. We are a little superstitious. We always head to the hospital for our deliveries with zero baby stuff. The nurses always ask, "Do you have the baby's first outfit?" I always respond, "Sure let's see what you got." I am prepared for everything in our life, except for having babies.

LESSON

Being Prepared

As a parent, you should think everything through. Don't fear everything through. Life doesn't always go as planned, and with kids, it rarely does. So get prepared, and when shit hits the fan, you will probably be able to handle it. I wasn't afraid of moving to our new house while I was on bed rest; I was prepared. I am not afraid when we fly with four kids, I am prepared. So when you are planning anything for your family, prepare. Educate yourself. If you are getting on an airplane with little ones, have extra clothes and diapers—and then have extras for the extras. AND ALWAYS HAVE EXTRA CLOTHES FOR YOURSELF. If you are going to a party and taking the little ones, take their pajamas too. Get them ready for bed before you get home. If your child's class has been coming down with the flu and you think it's making a stop at your house next, put a bucket and some towels in your car and near your child's bed. Like I said: be prepared, not scared. If some sort of outbreak rears its head in your neck of the woods, call your doctor and ask if you and your children are up to date on your vaccines. If you are heading out of town, put a hold on your mail. Just get prepared. As soon as you get the school supply list, take your kids shopping for their supplies. Just get it done. When your kiddo gets invited to a party, go get the gift. Don't get it on your way to the party. Teach your children to get their school bags and sports gear packed and by the door the night before. Get prepared; life is so much easier if you are prepared. And you will be teaching your children to be prepared too.

The move went great, with a couple of hiccups. Starting Friday, I went to the hospital once a day for three hours to be monitored. I couldn't drive because of the bed rest. So I had to have people drive me. We were told to be ready at a minute's notice to deliver Harvey. I made it to Monday and Harvey was born, happy and healthy. The delivery was fine. But that night, our sitter staying at the house with the kids called my cell phone at 9:00 p.m. because one of the carbon monoxide detectors was going off. I was screaming into the phone to get the kids out of there. I was also yelling at David to go home. He didn't want to leave me alone at the hospital. And I was dialing 911 on the landline from my hospital bed. (Read about Parker Lofgren, the brother of one of my best friends, and you will see why I was freaking out.) I had the fire department and the natural gas company show up at our house to check everything out. I had to threaten to divorce David to get him to leave Harvey and me at the hospital to check on the kids and the house. It was a zoo.

I spent my first night in the hospital alone with Harvey. And the nurses were on some screwed up schedule, so they weren't managing my pain meds. I had to get out of bed by myself after a C-section to go into the halls to flag a nurse down to get my meds. And the hospital was under construction at night, so it was very noisy. It was a terrible hospital stay. The hospital is normally great after you have a baby. You are waited on hand and foot, and your baby sleeps and sleeps. The nurse comes in to tell you when to feed. They deliver food to you in bed. It's great! But this time I just wanted to go home.

When they went to circumcise Harvey, his penis was not fully developed. So they basically had to leave the beginning of the circumcision unfinished. He would need surgery in si months to finish his circumcision. At every turn, some cu ball was being thrown at us. Seven days after moving into our house, we came home after a horrible rainstorm and the basement had flooded because a gutter overflowed. We just looked at each other, laughed, and cleaned up the water.

LESSON

Don't Sweat the Small Stuff

Don't sweat the small stuff. I suck at this, but I am learning. I think I find a little bit of joy stressing about this or that. But I have learned over time that if you can't fix the problem, there is no point in making it bigger and stressing out about it. Or, if you can fix it, then start fixing it. There was nothing we could do about me being on bed rest except wait. When the gutter overflowed into our basement, we cleaned up the mess. Parenting will make you a frazzle-bag one way or another. You will either be a total stress-ball about a sleep schedule, what school your kiddo goes to, or how many bites of broccoli your little one has. Whatever it is, there is absolutely no way anyone can get out of parenting without being frazzled about something. So turn the energy of your "frazzlement" into something ... either solve your problem, accept it, or ignore it. And if you can't do one of those, get counseling. Do you ever see those moms who are beyond stressed? Their kids aren't far ourself some help!

nree kids of my own, a stepson, and four e C-section, I was home-bound for six weeks

and couldn't lift anything but Harvey. What do an
this situation? Scream as loud as you can for help. Ou
sitter was on around the clock; she didn't drive, so w
cabs come to the house to pick her up from our house, take
her home to walk and feed her dog, and then bring her back.
My good friend Carrie basically moved in. I knew that after
Harvey was born I would need even more help. So I got on
the computer and made an Excel spreadsheet with a twenty-
four-hour, six-week schedule of friends who could come help
me with the kids, moving in, driving, and taking care of the
dogs. I took help from *anyone*! I even had an old co-worker's
wife come over. Once again, I was fully prepared. David was
around, but free to attend meetings and work stuff as he needed. Despite the craziness of it all, I think my six weeks went
pretty smoothly. I don't remember too much of it.

Jump ahead three years ...

Raising kids is a great job. I think I do okay at it. Keeping our
schedule organized and on time is very important to me. One,
it keeps me on track, and two, it keeps my kids on track. I
am working very hard to teach our kids about time management. There are three steps to this process. First, and most
importantly, is to keep myself on time. I do a great job at that.
Second is to teach our kids to get themselves organized and get
their stuff ready for school and their activities on time. Lastly, I
keep my kids "in the know" about what our schedule is. Each
morning I tell them what our day looks like. On the weekends, I have a list of what needs to get done around the house
for chores and what activities we have planned. Because Ian's
schedule involves more independence, I take him aside on

Fridays and let him know what we are up to, what obligations he has, and when I would suggest he tackle his homework. My goal since he started homework has been to teach him *not* to wait until the last minute to get his assignments completed.

I do not over-schedule our family. Yes, all of our children do activities, just not too many. All of our children have friends over and go to friends' homes, but just not too many. I work to under-schedule our life. I like big gaps of freedom in the day. I like evenings when David and I have nothing planned. And because I get all of my housework and family organizing done early in the morning, I can really enjoy these gaps of freedom. I also feel like we are teaching our children to enjoy their free time, and to also put their noses to the grindstone when it's time to work.

LESSON

Stick with It

One weekend, I told Ian he should have his homework done Saturday before he hung with his friends, because he had two soccer games Sunday and we had plans that night. Here is a key point, do not ever, ever, ever give your child an ultimatum you cannot follow through on. If you can't stick to your guns, don't try to get your kids to. Anyway, that Saturday I watched Ian screw off all day. He slept 'til noon, watched TV, played soccer, watched more TV, and didn't touch his homework. I did not nag, I did not remind, I did not mention our deal. At 7:30 p.m. that night, he said Jim was on his way over and they were going to see a movie. I said, "Great, after your homework is done." Ian was furious.

And he should have been; he screwed up. Kids rarely get mad at themselves, so Ian got mad at me. I let it go for a bit until he got out of hand, and then I said I would send Jim home and end his plans if he wanted to continue on with his attitude. Jim arrived a few minutes later, Ian got started on his homework, Jim waited, and they left for a movie later. That night I received this text from Ian:

> I'm really honestly sorry how I acted earlier. You were right to make me finish this tonite so that it would be off my back for the rest of the break. I was just frustrated at myself for not finishing it earlier an I wanted to see the movie. I'm sorry I love you

They get it, folks. They get the lessons. They need the lessons. They need the structure. They don't need to be caged, but they need boundaries and rules to keep them safe, sane, and in check. I kept my cool through the whole ordeal with Ian. I had the upper hand—and I should have, as I'm the parent. I'm not a dictator, exactly. But when I lay down a rule, it's one I know I can stick to. My rules are thought out. And they are thought out from my perspective. Will I be able to follow through with this punishment or rule? Do I ever worry about whether or not one of our kids is upset because they have gotten in trouble? I do not. What I think about is whether or not the punishment fits the crime. In Ian's case, the punishment certainly fit the crime. He didn't do a damned thing all day, and because of that, his social time got dented. I didn't warn him all day about it because he needs to learn to manage his life; he needs to learn what his responsibilities are, as well as time management. I don't want to be a meddling parent and I'm usually not. But if my kids don't get done what I ask them to get done, then it will start affecting their lives, not mine.

If I were you, I would be wondering why I gave Ian rules around his homework that weekend. Over the past few weekends, I had seen Ian stressed on Sunday nights staying up very late to complete his schoolwork. I asked him if he would like me to help him manage his time better. He said he would give my ideas a try. Although we had a little rough patch following my homework timeline, Ian was thrilled on Sunday night to be relaxing instead of staying up late doing homework.

ANOTHER LESSON

Pause

As for the little ones, I have to pause before I discipline them. They seem to send my temper to the moon. So to get myself calm when I see, hear, or find a child misbehaving. I tell the child to "have a seat" (usually on a stair). As my child is kicking and screaming and melting down on the stair, I can walk away, get calm, think about the situation, and come up with a reasonable punishment if one is needed. Once, on a hike, one of our children (I won't name names) deliberately tripped the other one. David was livid, as was I, in addition to being sad for the kid who was tripped. It's tough to punish your kid in the woods, but we did. We took the offender's shoes and socks for about five minutes of the hike. We told him if he couldn't use his feet the right way then he didn't deserve shoes and socks.

That same child fell off his tricycle the next day and was pretty mad. He stood up crying, picked up a ball, and threw it as hard as he could at one of the dogs. Wow! The tripping incident was still fresh in my head. I told him to have a seat—I was furious. I wanted to let that kid have it, I wanted to scream in his face, I wanted to throw the ball at him. Instead, I walked away. I got calm, I gathered my thoughts, I remembered his age and that he was probably hurt from falling off the bike, and I came up with a plan. I got a ball and asked him if he would like me to throw it at him. He said no. I asked why, and he said because it would hurt. I had him go outside and play fetch with the dogs for 50 throws. Five throws he probably would have enjoyed, but fifty was a lot. You should have seen the dogs, they were *so* happy.

It's hard to punish kids. It's hard to do it right. It's hard to not lose your shit. My punishments were not fun to administer, but I think they fit the crimes, and they worked. The little offender learned a lesson both times. What I didn't do was take something completely random away, or scream at him, or worse. I didn't take his stuffed animal or Legos or any future playdates away. I did not take away something that I thought would really stir him up. So make sure your punishments fit the crime, and keep your words to a minimum. When you are mad, you are generally searching your brain for something harsh to say. It's always a waste of your breath and very shaming. Say less.

Raising this many kids is hard sometimes. My kids realize there is only one of me and four of them. Our kids don't know I have twins on the way—nor do our friends. David and I are in shock. The doctor begged us to put two embryos in on our third IVF transfer. I said, "Let me think about this for a second … fuck no!" Well, guess whose embryo split? At my first ultrasound, there was one healthy embryo and a blood clot. At our second ultrasound, I thought the blood clot had grown. Twins were *not* on my radar. IVF embryos splitting happens 1% to 2% of the time. I mentioned to the doc that the blood clot had grown, and David said, "That's not a blood clot, that's another baby." I really don't have much to say about this turn of events, except that I am still in shock. I would like to finish this book before the babies are due (on July 24, 2015). So I am not sure I will be sharing my twin experience with you. And after they are born, I don't imagine having another second of time to myself … I will be taking care of six kids, three dogs, a busy husband, and our house. Yikes!

With four kiddos, our kids have become very self-sufficient. Years ago I read a book about raising kids with confidence, and it changed my parenting. When I first started dating David, I thought being the best parent meant to do absolutely everything you could for your children. God, was I sorely mistaken; that is the perfect way to raise spoiled brats. I remember it so well. I was probably four chapters into the book about raising kids with confidence when, one night, Ian was upstairs in the bathroom. He had just gotten out of the shower and was screaming at the top of his lungs for me to hike upstairs and bring him a towel. He had forgotten to grab one for himself. I turned up the radio and ignored him. The book had taught me that if I was to hike upstairs to grab Ian a towel, he would have no reason to remember to grab his towel before his shower next time. And all of a sudden, I would have yet another duty added to my list: fetching towels for those who had just finished their daily showers. I learned that day that if a kid is capable, he can certainly do for himself. And my parenting was changed forever. My parenting philosophy has been one of delegating responsibility to those who are capable.

LESSON

Empowering Your Kids

Empower your kids and they will grow up with a great sense of confidence. You will raise children who can conquer the world. They won't be afraid to try new things or meet new people. So start at home and stop doing for your children what they can do for themselves. All of our children make and pack their own lunches, put away their laundry, work around the house, make their beds, clear their plates from the table, dress themselves, get their school bags ready for school, do their own homework, clean up after themselves, buckle themselves into the car, unpack their bags at school and after school at home—the list goes on and on and on.

Ian has been given an allowance since he was eight years old. At age ten we told him he was to spend his own money for movies, toys, meals out with friends, and any other odds and ends. Ian's freshman year of high school, we gave him a lump sum of money at the beginning of the year. The money was for him to pay for clothing, cleats, haircuts, movies, books, rentals on On Demand, and to save for a car. He even took his own money on a soccer trip to California. Yes, we put him on a plane with his soccer team and did not hand him a penny. When I picked him up from the airport after his soccer trip to California, he told me that sales tax sucks. I told him I disagreed, and he asked why. We talked on and on about the advantages and disadvantages of sales tax. I am pretty sure we would have not had that conversation about sales tax if he was freely spending my money in California. Ian is now paying for himself. Our plan was for him to learn about money management. Well ... it has worked better than we expected. A month into school, I asked him why he was always packing his lunch. He said because it was expensive to buy lunch at school. When he paid for his first haircut, he wasn't happy about it or the price. Ian is learning about money; he will not head off to college clueless about the value of what's in his wallet.

We were chugging along, four kids, two dogs (we sadly lost our two black labs to old age). I had two days a week to myself: Ian was in school full-time and the little ones were in school two days a week. I felt like my head was finally coming out of the clouds; it was the first time in four years I was not pregnant or nursing. I had my body back. We were grooving. We had some great rules laid down for our family. One of my favorites ...

LESSON

Traveling with Toys

We do not bring toys anywhere. Nope. We head out of town every summer for two weeks; I do not pack one single toy. We go out to dinner and we do not bring toys. We head to the park and don't bring toys. We go to friends' houses and do not bring toys. I want our children engaging in the world around them, not buckled down in their own world playing with a toy from home. Yes, this means sometimes I am on duty a little more than I would be if we had packed a few toys. But that's my job, and I love my job. I do not use toys to keep our children occupied. And we never have to return anywhere to find a lost toy.

ANOTHER LESSON

Screen Time

We also do not let our younger children watch TV. So you won't find our kids engaged in a movie, TV show, or video game at our house or while we are out and about. Our children are out enjoying this world, talking with people, running around, and playing. They aren't sitting around melting their brains. They are using them, checking out what's going on around them.

Over the next summer (2013), life was good. It was easy. I wanted another baby, and so did David. My tubes were tied after Harvey. It was recommended by the doctor, and since I'm not one to ignore doctor's orders, I didn't really think about it. David did. He kept asking me, are you sure you want to have your tubes tied? Are you sure? I just thought, tie my tubes, whatever. I didn't look into it; I didn't talk to anyone about it. I just signed the paperwork and did it. Well, two years later, I wished I hadn't. David and I made an appointment with an OB/GYN in town who I knew a few friends had used. She had been aggressive in both of my friends' cases. She came into the room, and we introduced ourselves and told her why we were there. Without a pause she said she would have had more children if it wasn't for her divorce. That was my first endorsement. She told us she could reverse my tubal ligation, but that wasn't 100%. So she recommended IVF (in vitro fertilization). We were kinda in shock, but we called and made an appointment with the IVF doctor she recommended.

With our history and my regular menstrual cycle, it seemed like a pretty simple process. I take some drugs so that my body will produce more than one egg, and David steps into a private room for his fancy work. We really wanted this whole process to be very private. We asked to take the class about the medications privately. So we sat on our porch with David's laptop and watched a video to learn all about the medications and the next couple of months. It all seemed pretty simple and David had agreed to give me all my injections. Did I mention David has multiple sclerosis and gives himself weekly injections? I felt like I had a pro at home.

We bought all the meds. The first thing was for me to figure out when I ovulate and go into the office daily for bloodwork. They would call daily in the afternoon with my numbers. I would answer the phone, listen, and pretend I understood. Then one day I was at a friend's birthday party. I got my daily call and I had to go home and give myself a shot immediately. David was in a meeting he couldn't leave. I left the party, went home, and locked myself in the laundry room, where we had the medicines stored in the fridge. I called the nurse back, and she walked me through mixing, filling the syringe, and stabbing myself. I did it and was pretty proud.

But then I started thinking about it all. The thought of stabbing myself was really scary and I started to wonder what the fuck I was getting myself into. Was this really necessary? What the fuck did I just inject myself with? I didn't research any of the medications. I knew if I read one side effect I would end up with it. So I just did what I was told. I quit working out as my delicate belly began growing eggs. I went in daily to measure how big my follicles were. Each follicle contained an egg. Every time the doctor would count to about fifteen or so—on each ovary—and say there were plenty. I didn't question the numbers. Then it was time to go in and have the eggs sucked out of each follicle. They gave me a sedative, and when I woke up, the doctor told me he had gotten forty-one eggs. I was a record breaker, especially for my age (I was forty). The most he had retrieved at one time was forty-three, and that patient was twenty-three years old. He was shocked. David was patting me on the back like I won a sporting event. I was loopy and wanted to go home.

Because of my age and since we had kicked nature out the door when we decided to do IVF, we decided to have all the embryos genetically tested. Out of those forty-one eggs, we ended up with thirteen embryos. After the testing, we had eight healthy female embryos. I was in shock on the phone with the embryologist. I felt like I had lost 33 babies. I thought of all the women who only get a few eggs and their odds. It was strange. But the embryologist was very happy with the results. She said women are lucky to get two or three embryos. So I was off to a good start. But I wasn't feeling well.

At Thanksgiving I felt horrible. I didn't eat any turkey; I forced myself to have pumpkin pie because it's my favorite. I went to bed early, and the next day I was miserable. We called the doctor and they had us come in. I had ovarian over-stimulation from producing 41 eggs. My stomach was distended and I was miserable. I had to wait it out. It was awful and I was so scared to be feeling that bad. It was like having the flu, strep, and pneumonia, and it was caused by messing with my body's natural program. So I was pissed at myself and pissed at the doctor and questioning our decision to spend all this time and money for me to feel like I was dying. Finally, after about five days, my stomach got smaller. But I still wasn't feeling better. I had to go to the ER. I had some bloodwork done and my pancreatic enzymes were elevated. So I had a full body CAT scan. I had pancreatitis. I didn't have it bad, but it felt like I did. I felt horrible, and it was painful all over my mid region. I was sent home with pain meds, but no explanation as to why I had pancreatitis. I'm not a drinker and I don't have a gallbladder—two common causes of pancreatitis. After a few days, I was worse. I made an appointment with our family primary care doctor. She walked in the room, looked at me, and walked out. She came back 10 minutes later and had a room for me in the hospital; I was admitted for observation.

I was scared shitless, but at least I had a break. Taking care of the house, kids, and dogs while I was feeling like shit and totally stressed out about my health was taking its toll on me. And David kept having to leave work to run me to the doctor or pick up kids or whatever. It was taking a toll on his work life.

So David walked me over to my room at the hospital, tucked me in, and quickly left to start picking up kids from school. The nurse came in immediately to get me all squared away and give me some meds for the pain. I just broke down. I was so scared, so tired, in so much pain, missing David and the kids, and again wondering why the fuck David and I weren't just happy with our four kids. I was feeling so greedy and spoiled. But I knew I had to focus on relaxing and getting my health back. What was done with the IVF was done; I couldn't go backwards.

LESSON

Don't Stress

Try not to stress about what you can't fix. I couldn't fix much lying in that hospital bed. So I just leaned into it, enjoyed the pain medicines, watched TV, and relaxed. I gave my brain, body, and soul a 36-hour vacation. Every second was needed.

The day after getting out of the hospital, I met with a pancreas specialist. His office was not in my favorite part of town. I was concerned, but he came recommended and was covered by our insurance. I walked out of his office feeling better but not great, constantly thinking about those eight embryos waiting to make a home in my uterus. The thoughts were just awful, and way more than we had ever anticipated. It was all so overwhelming.

LESSON

Slowing Down

You can't always be great at your job. I was really struggling to parent our kids. I had been sick for six weeks. I had the embryos to constantly think about and four kids to take care of and love, and dogs, the house, my husband, and most importantly, myself to take care of. It was very hard to be patient with and kind to our kids when I was struggling so much inside. I had to slow our life way, way down. I had to listen to and pay attention to my body. I had to do only what I could do. This is where a pause came in so handy for me. I had to pause every time I was about to face conflict, no matter who it was with. I had to slowly think through every situation. I learned during that time to slow it all down, way down. No need to kill myself over scheduling us. I also learned not to let my guard down with the kids. I kept their bedtime and responsibilities in line. Once I was better, I didn't want to reteach and retrain everybody. So, although I was a mess inside, I kept the kids on track, and that kept my workload down. Yes, it was very hard to keep my cool, and oftentimes I didn't. But we all survived.

I finally got through pancreatitis. The specialist's wife had had two children via IVF. So he was familiar with the process. The cause could have been all the hormones elevating the fat in my blood, but we did an endoscopy to be sure. There was a nick in my pancreatic duct that also could have been the cause. I will never know. The good thing was that I was getting better, and fast.

With my health back in check, it was time to consider an embryo transfer. We had to finish what we started. So I scheduled my embryo transfer. Bingo, first try, we transferred one embryo and I was pregnant. I was excited and we told everyone. At my first doctor's appointment there were two embryos; the single embryo had split. At my second appointment, there was only one embryo. I was sad, but I was still pregnant and was happy. I grew quickly; my body knew what to do. All was good. We told the kids and they were excited. David was happy, and I was due in October. Right before Teddy's birthday, we had our 16-week appointment. The little Doppler the doctor uses to hear the heartbeat had dead batteries. So the doc brought in the ultrasound and there on the screen was the image of a dead baby girl in my belly. I was watching the screen. And I saw her. She was just lying there, still. There wasn't anything moving in my belly, no fluid, no jerky arm or leg movements, nothing. I screamed my head off. I wanted her out. I feel bad saying that now, but to know you have something dead in your body—and that it's your daughter—is terrible. It's surreal. It's horrible. And the worst part was to think that she may have been suffering at some point and I didn't even know it. I wasn't able to help her or hold her with my arms. I was a wreck. David was crying. We didn't know what to do. The doctor said she could perform a D&C the next morning.

So we went home.

As we walked in the door, the kids all came running up with hugs, as they normally do when we come home. Our babysitter had fixed dinner. We all sat down to eat. It was life as usual, but with a dead baby girl in my belly.

We arranged for friends to take the kids to school the next morning, and David and I left early for the hospital. I don't remember saying much during that period. Carrying a dead baby girl in your belly leaves you speechless. And, of course, again, I was back to thinking about why the fuck we entered into IVF. But we did.

We got to the hospital and the anesthesiologist walked in to check my armband and confirm my name, date of birth, and procedure. He confirmed the first two and then asked if I was at the hospital for an abortion. Oh Jesus! David stood up ready to swing at the guy. I started crying for the fiftieth time in a 24-hour period. We all recovered, and David didn't deck the guy … I kinda wish he had. An hour later, I woke up not pregnant. Three days later was Teddy's birthday party.

LESSON

Speaking Up

Speak up! I didn't want to discuss what had happened with anyone at Teddy's birthday, nor did I want to leave the house for about two weeks. So I told those closest to me what I needed to. I told David he had to change his work schedule to accommodate the kids' schedules because I was off duty. I asked David to send out an email to all of the guests at Teddy's party explaining what had happened and to please respect our privacy; we did not want to discuss the matter. With the help of many, many friends, I gave myself two weeks to rest my mind, soul, and body. I had to ask for a lot of help to make this happen. If you are going through a difficult time, ask for help from your friends and family. You deserve it. And your family deserves to have you take care of yourself.

Teddy's birthday went off without a hitch. He had a blast and I had a few well-deserved beers. We told the kids about the baby that evening. They handled it fine. Two months later, we did another IVF transfer. The embryo stuck, but only for a second, and I got my period. We waited another two months and did another transfer of one embryo, and here we are today. I'm pregnant with identical girls. That's my life so far.

The next section is a variety of information. You will find some more tips on parenting and a lot of tricks we do around the house. Please enjoy.

PART II
Manual

Basic Kelleher Rules

1. We love our children.
2. We really love our children.
3. Every parenting decision we make is to make their lives better and our lives better and easier.
4. Life is busy, so we try to enjoy every moment with them; even the worst diaper or tantrum is quality time with our kids.
5. No TV unless a kid is very sick or we are on an airplane.
6. We don't lift a finger to help our children unless we hear the word "please."
7. Our children are asked to leave the table whenever they have bad manners. They can eat at the next meal.
8. Our children are not force-fed. No "clean plate" rules here.
9. We can take our children into the best toy store in the world and not buy them a toy. There will not be a meltdown, a tantrum, or a lot of whining. They can just enjoy the experience.
10. Our children do a lot of work around our house. Two-year-olds can do chores.
11. Everyone writes thank-you cards. If you can color, you can write a thank-you card.
12. We do not budge on bedtime.
13. Our government does not negotiate with or bribe terrorists; we have the same policy for our children.
14. We do not ask our children to do things; we tell them to do things. Example: We do not say, "Can

you put your shoes on?" We instead say, "Please put your shoes on."

15. Lessons in life are generally taught through natural consequences. Our children are never told not to spill their milk; they learn by spilling their milk and then cleaning up the mess themselves.

Feeding You and Your Family

Feeding a lot of different taste buds can be challenging. Teaching your children healthy eating habits and how to enjoy a meal can be challenging too. Keep it simple, folks; offer food at meals and do not offer snacks in-between meals to children between the ages of two and five (unless there is a medical need). Try not to focus on what your children do or don't eat; focus on their manners. Offer your children food, nudge them to try it, and then let it go … there will be another meal. Do not battle with your children about food, just don't go there. Your children will *always* win the food battle, and although they may be sitting at your table crying as you are yelling at them to finish their peas, deep down they know they got this battle won. It will drive you crazier to have them stay at the table until they finish their food. Trust me, kids have amazing imaginations; they can sit for hours entertaining themselves and be smiling deep down because they know the score. They aren't finishing their peas and you can't make them. Your kids don't want to be hungry. Teach them to eat when their bodies tell them they are hungry.

Here are the food rules we live by. Our children will eat sushi, piles of steak, green salad, and happily try any food we put in front of them. And we do not need to scream at or bribe our children to do any of this.

Snacks

Below is a list of rules for snacking based on your child's age. This is put together by me, an outdated nutrition major. But I think it's a good guideline for those without any medical issues.

Babies until the age of 2

Omit the no snacking rule. Those little cuties need to eat *every three hours.* Your brain is made of mostly fat. Yep fat. So you want to plump those little babies up as much as you can. Eat, eat, eat!

SIDE NOTE

I breastfeed my children. Don't give up, ladies; there are a lot of resources to help you get this program right. It's hard and painful in the beginning. For the first six weeks, I screamed every time I fed Teddy. But I stuck with it. I fed him for three days after he was born, until my milk finally came in and continued on for one year. One of the understated benefits of breastfeeding is relaxation. When a mother is breastfeeding, she releases hormones to relax. Breastfeeding is a time for mommies to stop everything, sit down, relax and spend one on one time with their infant. If you can give breastfeeding a shot, you won't regret it.

Ages 2 to 4

This is a tough age, in a lot of ways. Lots of meltdowns, lots of misunderstanding, lots of everything. But on a happier note, there is a lot of learning at this age: potty training, talking, walking, sleeping. Children are beginning to manage their own needs, and eating is one of them. At age two, stop snacking. Stop offering your children food every hour on the hour. They don't need it.

Stop packing snacks on your way out the door. Stop offering your children food in-between meals. I understand packing food for an outdoor activity; our bodies need fuel. I get it. However, are you irritated when your kids don't eat at meals? Are you frustrated because your outings are consumed with your children asking you what other food you have in your bag? Stop snacking. Children's tummies are very small and don't require a lot of food. If you need a reference, curl your child's fingers into a fist; that is the size of his stomach. It is not very big. I do not offer snacks in our house. Allow your children to come to the meal table with an appetite; don't spoil that by offering them snacks after breakfast and school and then expect them to eat decent meals. Their bodies don't need that much food. In our house our children come to the table ready to eat. When they sit at the table, they stay there because they are hungry and they want food, and we expect them to stay at the table during mealtime. I never leave the house with snacks packed up.

Here are a few tips to get you on the no-snack bandwagon:

- There is access to food everywhere in the United States of America, so if you really need food, you can get it while you are out and about. Because of this, I do not leave the house with food. If my children really get in a jam and are hungry, I can buy them some food.
- Skipping snack packing saves me *tons* of time on my way out the door. I just grab my purse and the kids and go.
- Snacks tend to not be as healthy as meals. Generally, snacks are a bar or a bag of something—not a great nutrition program for you or your kids.
- If your kids do get hungry, they will be okay. It's good for your child to learn about hunger. A hungry child is more likely to try new foods than a child filled up on snacks. It's great for children to learn about their bodies, and to learn when their bodies do and do not need food. Obesity is a *major* problem and I think snacking is *major* contributor to the problem.

SIDE NOTE

When I am out and about, I always see the moms with their earth-friendly snack containers, following their kids around, trying to offer them food and drinks. These moms should grab a seat, chat with their friends, or read their books, and quit offering their children food. Trust me, your kids will tell you if they are thirsty or hungry.

Your children are going to ask you for food. That's okay. They are going to go through a huge transition when you remove snacks from their diet, and you need to get on board. It's gonna be tough if you have been a snacking family. If your kiddos ask for food, this could be because they see food, you started cooking dinner, you brought the groceries in, or they are truly hungry. Here's how you handle it:

- Smile and say, "We will have food at our next meal."
- If you get a tantrum, read the section on "have a seat."
- If your child begs, offer her a glass of water and ask her to pick out a cup. Have her sit at the table with a book to have the glass of water. That will get her out of your hair and get her thinking about something else.
- If she wants more after the water, ask her to help you do what you are doing, cleaning, cooking, etc.
- If she keeps at it, offer her a glass of milk. But the buck stops there: no food. A half-glass of milk should sufficiently fill up a child's belly.
- If your child's behavior gets really bad, you have created a snack monster. And if your snack monster does not eat good meals and you find yourself begging her to eat during meals, you must get on board with this new plan. Be patient; in a week or so your child will be on the no-snack program.

If you have to pack snacks because you are going hiking or to sports or whatever, don't let your kids see you pack up a bunch of snacks. If they see it, they will ask for it. If they don't, they may not ask for it. And if they don't ask for snacks, guess what? Their little bodies don't need 'em! Don't think I am trying to starve anyone here; I most certainly am *not*.

If you have a child diagnosed with any sort of blood sugar disorder or medical issues, then you are on a different program that is hopefully monitored by a physician. Please do not diagnose this for your child. Go to the doctor and let him do the appropriate tests. You may think your child suffers from low blood sugar because he perks up after you give him food. Your child may just be tired and need an earlier bedtime—so please, please, please do not diagnose medical issues for your child. Thank you.

Ages 5 to 11

Unless your child has weight or health issues, a light snack after school or camp or sports can be necessary. Kids go hard, very hard. Again, *please do not offer your children a snack*; let them ask for it (an opportunity for your children to learn to speak up if they need something). I'll say it again, don't offer your children food. Think of it this way, if you offered to buy your child a toy, he would say "yes" every time. So if you offer food, your child will accept the offer and then most likely not eat a great "next" meal.

As for what you give your kids for a snack—who cares? In other words, don't worry about it too much. When time permits, I cut up a bunch of vegetables and put those out. If I don't have time, I give them something they will eat. It's a snack, folks. Teach healthy eating habits during meals. Don't stress out over what your children snack on. It's probably one-tenth of their caloric intake for the day. No need to put a lot of stress on snacks; just give some nuts, a bar, pretzels, fruit, string cheese, half a sandwich. Treat them to a shake at McDonald's. Who cares? Have fun with it, it's a snack. I know you are probably thinking, "I should make every calorie count; I should make it all nutritious." No. Just get food in their bodies when they need it. When you are sitting down at the table for a good meal, then you can talk about nutrition and why food is important.

Ages 12 to 20 ... The Growth Spurts

These come fast and hard. Starting at age 13, Ian couldn't get enough sleep or food. If he could have done both at once, he would have.

Get ready, cuz your kids are going to start eating like you have never seen before. If your children do not have a weight problem (high or low), just let them open up the pantry and go for it. They need all the calories they can get. So let them eat whenever they want. Ian and I talk a lot about what foods he would like to eat for his "fourth meal" (the one after dinner). Sometimes I will make a pound of pasta and leave it in the fridge for him and his friends to heat up. Sometimes frozen burritos are a good snack, or cereal. I have found Ian isn't really interested in preparing his fourth meal; he wants something quick. Again, I don't put a lot of emphasis on healthy eating for the "fourth meal"—it's just a big evening snack enjoyed by all teenagers.

Age 20 and Up

If you are an adult and you have weight issues, chances are you snack. Healthy snacks are good, but not great. You aren't growing up anymore, just out. A little snack after exercise is understandable, but anything other than that isn't necessary. Have a cup of tea or a coffee with skim milk. Sorry, folks, but we just don't need the calories we used to.

Serving Your Family Food

After the age of two, children do not eat a lot of food. Sometimes they won't be hungry at breakfast, lunch, or dinner. I beg you: please allow your children to listen to their bodies about whether or not they are hungry. From what I understand, starvation is a horrible feeling; I would not know. If you are reading this book, your children probably will not feel what it is like to starve. Teach your children to taste foods because foods are good and fun to try, and because they are fuel for children's bodies. Allow your children to not eat very much at a meal because their bodies don't need it and they are listening to their bodies. Remember: dehydration will kill you before starvation.

Sitting at the Kelleher Table

Here's how we sit down for dinner at our house:

1. The kids are getting hungry, so I tell them to have a seat at the table as I am finishing up dinner. They can grab a book or magazine (I keep a stack of books right next to the table in the kitchen for this purpose.)
2. When dinner is ready, we trade whatever they are reading for a plate of food. I tell them everything that

is on the plates. If I have cut up apples on their plates, I tell them that too, even if they know what it is.

3. I bring extra milk, water, and food to the table before I sit down. I try to keep the number of times I have to get up to a minimum. I also will only refill a glass of milk or water (or whatever beverage the children are having) *after* they have eaten some of the food on their plates. The kids can't fool me if they are trying to fill up on milk.

4. After we are all seated at the table, everyone can start eating.

5. Our kids need to sit at the table and speak at a decent level and with a decent tone of voice.

6. They need to use their silverware for what it's intended to be used for: eating. Not sword fights, drumsticks, or anything else they come up with.

7. The children need to not bang their plates or cups on the table.

8. They need to pass the napkins or anything when asked.

9. They need to ask for seconds using the word "please."

10. When they have finished eating, they ask to be excused and then clear their dishes from the table.

11. If dessert is an option, then they help themselves to that.

If any, and I mean *any*, of these rules are not followed, dinner is over for that child. I say, "You are done. Please clear your plate." That child doesn't get any more food, he doesn't get dessert, and he doesn't get to continue sitting with the family during dinner. It's an opportunity to have a nice, warm meal served to them; I want them to respect that. My children have missed a lot of meals because of poor manners and behavior at the table. They are all still alive and all still making their marks on their growth charts.

More Rules About Sitting at the Family Meal Table

Like I said above, your children should start table manners around age two. You have stopped snacks now and your children should be coming to the dining table with hungry little bellies. You say you don't sit down for meals. Come again? Sit down for your meals with your family. The dining room table is where it all happens. Cook the dinner, defrost it, or have it delivered and sit at the table. Yes, I know you have to get up many times to get seconds, to wipe a nose, or whatever. All those ups and downs will be gone one day, just like your kids. So enjoy it all while it lasts.

SIDE NOTE

There are a lot of studies about the benefits of sitting down to enjoy a meal together as a family. The benefits are huge! I'll let you look them up and be amazed for yourself.

Anyone and everyone who is at your home during mealtime has a seat at the table. I can't tell you how many contractors and guests sit down with us to eat a meal. I even had a guy for gay marriage who knocked at the door join us for dinner. If you are here, you are eating! I don't worry if I don't have enough food; I'll throw some cheese and crackers on the plate, cut up an apple, throw some chips in a bowl. Who cares; just rally everyone to the table.

If your child is a wild one at the table, buckle him in. If you don't have one of those chairs you can buckle him in with, use a belt and strap him in with that. You may need to ignore the screams for a day or a couple of weeks. Think about the payoff. Picture my four kids sitting down to the table eating, behaving, and clearing their plates when the meal is over. Your child is capable; you just need to be a good, strong leader. And don't feel bad about belting your child in (even if they are six, seven, or eight years old). You buckled him into a highchair for years. He buckles himself into the car. It's just for safety ... at least that's what I tell our kids.

This is the most important rule about feeding your family. Serve everyone the same food. Even if you know your kid doesn't like Brussels sprouts, put them on her plate anyway. Your child must get used to having food on her plate that she doesn't like. Have you ever sat down with a bratty nine-year-old that freaks out because of the parsley on her plate? Let's avoid that and let your child get used to "yucky" food on her plate. And ... you never know. Your child might be inclined to taste that yucky food one day. So keep giving her the opportunity.

If you have one of those kids who can't have different parts of the meal touching, you made a mistake long ago ... let's get it fixed. If you have a child that is trying this out, do not entertain it. I repeat: do not entertain this. Do not re-plate your child's food, do not scoot the food over, just say, "I'm sorry." If the child cries about it again, say, "I'm sorry." Just be a broken record and keep saying you are sorry. Don't tell him the food will taste the same; he will not hear what you are saying. Just keep saying, "I'm sorry your food is touching." And if he won't drop it, tell him to clear himself and his plate from the table and tell him that you will be serving breakfast in the morning. You worked hard to cook or pay for your dinner; you do not need anyone disrespecting any portion of the meal.

A lot of nutrition books will tell you to put everything you are serving in serving dishes and put those on the table. Then everyone can serve themselves. I have not done this yet because I don't want to have the extra dishes to clean. Shame on me! Maybe one day.

If your children can walk, they can clear their own plates from the table. Yes, you are going to have tons of spills. That's okay. Hand your kid a rag and have her clean up the spills herself. Don't tell your kiddo not to spill; it will not stop any messes. Let your kiddo learn that her milk will spill if she does not carry it carefully. Natural consequences! Do not hover over your child as she walks her plate of grapes over to the sink. Let her do it herself; she can and she will. Just say, "Thank you for clearing your plate," or, "I'm sorry you spilled your grapes; please clean them up."

Give your children dessert! Everyone loves dessert, and kids especially do. So let's celebrate and have a yummy little treat after a good family meal. I let our kids choose something small out of the pantry. Sometimes I let them choose a piece of fruit for dessert. But every night, they get a little treat, and they really enjoy it. And—drum roll, please—it buys me 10 minutes to clean up the kitchen before the bedtime routine.

Lunch

Let's kick this off with a bang: if your child forgets to bring his lunch to school, *do not bring it to him.* If you bring it to him, then why would he need to remember it the next day, and the day after that? Let your kids scrounge from their friends for food. They will survive. Yes, our children have gone without lunch—many times. And I start young. Teddy forgot his lunch for school at age four. The teachers gave him some animal crackers. I knew he forgot it; I saw it in the fridge when I was adding a little more creamer to my coffee after I had dropped everyone off at school. Did I feel bad I wasn't hopping in the car to bring him his lunch? Sure, but I knew he wasn't going to starve. He would be fine. And he was. Guess what Teddy said when I picked him up: "I'm never forgetting my lunch again. Those crackers didn't fill me up." There would be no way for him to learn that lesson if I had brought him his lunch. Natural consequences.

A few weeks later, Teddy forgot his lunch again. I saw his backpack sitting on the floor before we left for school. I threw him a bone and told him to chat with me while I was helping Harvey get his shoes on, and we were sitting right next to his backpack. He sat down right by his backpack and still forgot it with his lunch inside. The school called twice to ask me to bring him lunch; I didn't answer. I checked the messages to make sure there wasn't an emergency. There wasn't; the school just wanted me to bring him his lunch. This is a tough one, but it's big. Teach your children early to get their school stuff organized and ready for school. Please don't be that parent who brings your children lunches or homework, or your children will be screwed in college.

All of our children pack their own lunches for school—even the two-year-old. Yes, I am there to supervise, but I am not slaving over lunches. They are. I'm generally sitting at the table reading a magazine as they are packing and discussing their lunches. It's actually a pretty magical time for our children. They all come together working on a common goal for themselves. They help each other out, grabbing this or that. If one is making a bagel with cream cheese, I encourage them to see if anyone else wants one. They offer to grab bars or drinks for each other. There is a lot of teamwork and little fighting. Aside from the fantastic teamwork happening, there are other reasons the kids pack their own lunch:

- My kids can pack their own lunches, so they do.
- It's another way they can contribute around the house.
- Your children will get to know their way around a kitchen.
- Your children will learn how to feed and nourish their own bodies. If you are making your own food, you end up being more conscious about what you like to eat and, more importantly, how much you need to eat.
- If your children pack their own lunches, they are less likely to forget them in the morning.
- If your children pack their lunches they will eat them.
- Most importantly, it's empowering. And whenever you can empower you kids, you're doing wonders for them!

And if you do start this plan at your house, here's how it will mostly likely go:

1. Start by telling your children it's time to make lunches. I tell our children to put at least one healthy item

in their lunches. The rest is up to them. I guided them a bit in the beginning, making suggestions. Peanut butter and jelly tortilla roll-up, cheese and crackers, leftovers from dinner, frozen pizza—but for the most part, I sit back and let them choose everything.

2. If your kids are older and you tell them it's their job to make their lunches, you are going to get lots of pushback. So your older kids will probably need their hands held through this, and be reminded a lot. Don't give up or give in. Your kids are capable of making their lunches. They can do it, they should do it, and it will take one more job off your back.

3. Be prepared for the messy sandwiches, the kitchen getting destroyed, the kids eating while they make their lunches. Don't worry about it; think of the long-term goal: your children are learning to care for themselves.

4. In the beginning, this is going to take about 45 minutes per kid per lunch. I know, it's a lot of time, and yes, it's easier to just do it yourself. But don't. Just turn on the music, grab a magazine and cocktail, and assist your kids when they need it. Let them learn to do this. Send your children out in this world knowing how to feed themselves—and start with teaching them how to pack their lunches.

5. You will figure out the best time in your house for lunch making. Here are some suggestions: Right after school: if your kids have snacks after school, then they can snack and make their lunches all in one motion. After homework: you will probably get a lot of pushback on this because your kids are tired. Another time for your children to make their lunches is right before they go to bed; maybe they could have their

after-dinner treat (if that is an option in your home) while they pack up their lunches. I think the worst time to make lunch is before school. This is when Ian chooses to make his lunch, and it works great for him. It drove me nuts for years, but I kept my mouth shut because he was happily making his own lunch.

6. For the little ones, try a three-week plan. During the first week, you make their lunches with them nearby. During the second week, get them to help choose foods, make sandwiches, and so on. By the third week, you can be around to assist, but they should be doing the work.

7. Another thing you can do is have one of your kids (during family chore hour—you will read about that later) bag up a bunch of veggies and fruits so the kids can grab those during the week.

Give this a try, and give it three weeks! You will love it. And you will be empowering your kids!

Let's Sum Up Feeding Your Family

*   Hold up on the snacking. And if that doesn't work for your family, at least wait until your child has asked for food. Teaching your children to listen to their hunger is a very important lesson; let your children learn it.
*   When you serve your family food, tell everyone what it is and politely ask your children to try it. Do not get into a food battle with your children; you will lose.

- Expect and demand manners at your table. If you do not get them, politely ask your child to leave the table.
- Let your children have the opportunity to start packing their own lunches. They will enjoy being in charge of their lunch menu. When they pack their lunches, they are less likely to forget them. If they do forget them, you know what to do—let them take those yummy lunches to school the next day.

Plain Old Parenting

We are kinda old school at our house. We don't spank our kids. We are tough on them, but loving and *very* dependable. When I say "tough," I mean it; our punishments are not negotiated. Ruined clothing is not replaced from our bank accounts—our children can pay for new clothes to replace those they have lost or ruined; rude or disrespectful children are removed from their activities. Natural consequences are felt by our children, not buffered by us. If a child forgets to bring his homework to school, we do not bring it to him. The same goes for lunches, athletic equipment, and whatever else our children should be managing for themselves.

When I say we are dependable, I mean it. If Wiggy asks me to sew a button on her doll's clothing, I do it. I may not get to it right away, but I make sure I get it done, with her sitting by my side, helping me. If Ian asks for one of us to quiz him for an exam, we ask what time and we are there. If Teddy asks for us to attend his school mass with him, we do our best to make it happen. If Harvey wants to go to a school event and our schedule doesn't allow for it, I help him find a school family to take him. On that same note, if our children ask us not to attend a soccer game, school meeting, friend's birthday party, or something that does not require a parent, we respect their wishes. I want our children to know they can depend on us and trust that we will be there or not. We will not be here forever for our kids; I want to give them the biggest springboard I can for them to launch into their own lives. And we want those lives to be the best they can be.

They cannot launch into their own lives if I am doing everything for them. They cannot do that if I am going to pick up the messy pieces. I cannot step in front of my children's hurt feelings so they don't feel any pain. That's not the life I grew up in. I had some hard times in life. I don't want our kids to go through some of the tough times I did, but I do want them to go through life experiencing both good and bad. I didn't become a commodities trader (with a nutrition degree) or own a $100,000-a-year jewelry business or become the number one skier for my high school because my parents paved the road for me. No, I busted my ass to get to those places. And I smile a little bit every time I think of any of my accomplishments. I am one proud lady, and I should be. I want my children to be able to give themselves those same opportunities. I want our kids to have grit. And every single parenting move we do is creating it. Everywhere we go, we are told how well-behaved and happy our children are. It makes me proud, but I know there is still a lot of living I have to let them do, and I am excited and scared to let them do it. Let your children fail, let your children succeed, let your children cry, let your children get hurt (safely). It will all be very hard to watch, but your children will be stronger, better, more confident, and happier people the more you stay out of the way.

Independence

Give your children the opportunity to be independent. Let them do things for themselves. The more your children are able to take care of themselves, the more confident and self-sufficient they will be. And everything they learn to do for themselves will take one more job off your hands. Raising kids is a lot of fun and a lot of work. Your children are taking part in all the fun of being raised. Let them take part in some of the work too. Here are ways to help your children increase their independence. This section is broken into age groups.

Toddlers

- Purchase shoes and clothing they can put on themselves.
- Place stools all over the house so they can reach light switches, toys, books, jackets, etc.
- Let them put their toast in the toaster.
- Let them butter their own bread.
- Have them put their clothes away. If they can get clothes out of the drawer, they can put them in the drawer.
- Let them help you pack lunches. They can lay cheese on bread, they can put chips in bags, they can unzip lunchboxes, and they can grab juice boxes. They can really do a lot.
- Have them carry their own schoolbags to and from school. There is no need for any parent to carry their children's school bags. You are not a bellboy.
- Give them chores.

- Give them an allowance.
- Let them choose their own haircuts and color.

SIDE NOTE

When Wiggy was four, she left the house with her sheet, blanket, stuffy, lunch, and water bottle in her hands. She didn't want to take her backpack. She was dropping stuff everywhere on her way out the door. It took her three trips to get her stuff in the car. She proudly looked at me and said, "I'm not using my backpack today." I smiled and didn't say a word. When we got to school, she got out of the car and started grabbing her stuff. She dropped her stuffy in the dirt; she wasn't happy. She grabbed her sheet and blanket, and stuff just started falling everywhere. She asked me to help without saying "please." I didn't respond because she didn't say "please." She finally got everything balanced and carried it all into school on her own. When we got to her classroom, she looked up at me and said, "Tomorrow I'm using my backpack."

Think for a few minutes how much my daughter got to experience and teach herself with that incident—and I didn't open my mouth once. I knew it would be a disaster to carry all that stuff to school—but I'm 41 years old; I should know that. She was four. She had a plan, and she wanted to do it, and I let her. This is the way to teach our children, folks. Wiggy wasn't going to get hurt struggling to carry all this stuff. If you see opportunities for your children to come up with an idea on their own (even if you know it isn't going to work), keep your trap shut and let them go for it.

Ages Four to Nine

All of the above and …

- Let them get themselves ready for school. Let them get dressed, pack their bags, remember their homework and their lunches.
- Let them pick their own after-school activities.
- Let them do their own homework—*alone*.
- Let them call their friends or friends' parents to organize playdates.
- Let them plan their birthdays.
- Let them choose what is for dinner and help cook once in a while.
- Let them get ready for bed.
- Let them order their food at restaurants.

When I say "let them," what I am saying is, let your children have these opportunities. Yes, your children may stumble, they may be nervous to order their food, they may be pissed they have to do their homework without you sitting at the table with them. But just remember, when you "let" your children do these things, you are decreasing your workload and improving their lives. Your children can do these things. You are *not* at school with your children, and they are plugging away at their schoolwork without you. Your children can easily ask you for a glass of milk at home, so they can certainly ask a server at a restaurant. Let your children use their voices and their skills. Let them see they have the voices and skills to navigate this world. Let them build their independence and confidence.

Tweens, Ages Nine to Twelve

All of the above and …

- Let them be the people they are growing up to be.
- Celebrate their independent thoughts. When your children come up with an idea, listen and ask questions. Show interest in what they have to say.
- Celebrate their choices. If your child chooses to try something new—baking, a new sport, a new friend—celebrate her bravery.
- Let them call and schedule their own doctor's appointments. Give them all the information they need, times that work, address, insurance, etc., and let them make the call.
- Get them a phone; just give it with rules.
- Have them discuss issues with their teachers on their own.
- Have your tweens get themselves out of bed with an alarm.

Nine-year-olds can do a lot. Give your children the opportunity to be the people they are growing up to be. Yes, they will bitch and moan when you start giving them little opportunities to do for themselves. They will think it's a job to call and set up their playdate, but it's not. It's an opportunity for your children to do for themselves. Eventually, these little jobs will become the norm. So wade through the muck as you are adding to your child's workload; it will pay off in the long run.

Teens

All of the above and …

- Have them pay for their phones.
- Let them screw up. This the best time for kids to screw up.
- Let them date.
- Let them be in a bad mood.
- This is your last chance to really parent your child. Do a good job, do a kind job—but most importantly, let your kids do their jobs too.

Lots of folks—me included—fear their kids becoming teenagers. I think about my teenage years and cringe. I was your typical teenager. I started driving at 14 by stealing my friend's mom's car. I had sex at 15 because everyone else was having it. And I tried some drugs. I never got in much trouble and nothing ever got out of hand. I guess I was a "smart" teen. My mom, rest her soul, gave me a lot of freedom. The freedom was awesome, but she had to know where I was at all times. I could never ever be home past my curfew. And most importantly, I had to respect her. If I didn't follow the rules, my privileges were gone. I won't go on about my colorful teenage years—I will save that for my next book, *How To Raise a F*cking Teen*.

Getting Up and Out the Door

From the age of four, your children should have the opportunity to get themselves up and out of bed on their own.

"Why?" you ask. Well, why not? Your children can do it, and they should. It is not your job to go into your child's room and struggle with him to get out of bed. It is your child's job, and it will be his job for the rest of his life; he should learn to do it now. This is the beginning of learning time management and getting up and to where you need to be in the appropriate amount of time. You will not be in your child's college dorm to wake them up, right? Let your child learn these skills now. If your little ones sleep in and miss daycare, no biggie. But for your older children to sleep in during grade school or high school is a *huge* deal, and very stressful. He may even miss a test. He may miss the bus or ride to school. This is not the end of the world, but to him, it may seem like it is. Your children need to learn to deal.

When you are old and in a wheelchair and someone is changing your Depends, you can't be the one calling your child to make sure she is going to make it to work on time for the multi-billion-dollar presentation she has with her boss. So let her learn now. It's okay if your child feels a little or a lot of stress in the morning because she slept in, missed a test, or missed the bus. When else are your children going to learn stress management? And let's be real here; this isn't true stress. True stress is losing your job when you have a family to support, or getting a scary medical diagnosis. The best place to learn these lessons is at home, not in college, and not on the job. So start now.

When and if your children are late to school or activities, the natural punishment has happened. You are off the hook; you don't have to punish them. The stress your children feel racing around the house getting ready, the wrath they are going to get at school or work for being late will all happen without you opening your mouth. When you let your children live and make their own mistakes during these early stages of life, you are doing so many great things for them. You do not need to wear any of your children's responsibility. You do not need to be rushing around, stressed out too, and bitching at your children for being late. Let them deal with the problem they have created. Certainly, be polite and offer to help them, but that's it. You do not need to beat them up any more than they are already beating up themselves. It sounds harsh, and it is. But it doesn't mean you love your kids any less; you are training your kids for life. Your job as a parent is to train your children and rear your children for the lives they are going to face—not carry all of the responsibility for the hardships they face or create. Life is tough, folks; there are a lot of lessons out there. If we can teach a few of them to our kids now in the safety of our homes, guess how prepared our children will be for the real world? Think of all the times you have said to yourself, I wished I learned this long ago.

SIDE NOTE

One morning, Ian wasn't downstairs at his usual time of 7:10 a.m. I checked my calendar to see if he had late opening. He didn't. The clock kept ticking and no Ian. Finally, at 8:00 a.m. he came down, brushing his teeth and looking very confused. I looked at him and said, "Good morning." He said, "What time is it?" It was 8:05 a.m. He just stared at me. I asked if he would like some help. He said yes and ran back upstairs to get his stuff. This was not my problem; it was Ian's. Ian asked if I would call the school; I asked him to the dial the number and hand me the phone. I asked him what happened; he said he woke up with his alarm, looked at it, and rolled over and went back to sleep. I dropped him off at 8:30 a.m. (his school starts at 8:00 a.m.). He said he was probably going to get detention. Was it hard for me to watch the clock and know that Ian was sleeping in? You bet. It's tough to watch your kid fail. Here's the deal: I knew Ian was safe, and that is very important to me. But I knew he was going to be late. Sure, I could have run up to his room and gotten him up, but then the lesson would have been lost. I would have gotten involved and screwed it all up. Instead, I let him live his life. Life is hard. I would rather have my kids have their first hardships under my safe, loving roof.

A NOTE TO ALL PARENTS

Do not waste your time explaining to your children that something is for their own good. You are only trying to make yourself look and feel better. Parenting does not always feel good. Get used to it. It's okay. I know my husband doesn't feel good when he has to fire someone, but he has to do it for the sake of his company. You have to parent your children for the sake of their lives. You know it's the right thing; doing the right thing doesn't always feel great.

Going to Bed

Bedtime can be challenging. Give your family more time than you need for your bedtime routine. Think of it this way. Bedtime is the last mile of a marathon. Your children have been running mile after mile all day long, and now they are about to finish the race. You have been volunteering all day long, handing out water and encouragement throughout the race. Everyone is exhausted and wants to hit the finish line at top speed, but it's impossible. Give yourself plenty of time to finish. Don't rush the bedtime process. It's like trying to sprint at the end of a marathon; your body feels like a wet noodle. You and your children feel the same at the end of the day. So slow down, chill out. If your children enjoy a bath or shower, give them plenty of time to enjoy it. Have your children grab their pajamas, diapers/Pull-Ups, and loveys before their bath time.

If you read to your children in the evening, or if your children read to themselves, figure out how long you will be reading. Ten minutes, twenty minutes; whatever it is, that is the maximum time you will be reading. Do not finish the book; do not read the book again, do not start a new book. If your allotted amount of time has ended, mark your spot in the book and continue reading there the following evening. Stick to your guns here. Keep it simple, "I'm sorry, but we are done reading for the night." And if you need to, repeat and repeat as you are walking to your children's bedrooms. As you are walking away, your children will follow because they want to continue begging you to keep reading. This is great because you are both headed in the right direction: to their beds. And you are calmly repeating, "I'm sorry, but we are done reading for the night."

If your little tiger doesn't follow you, that's okay too. Just scoop up that little one and gently carry her into her room. Ask if she would like to crawl into her bed herself or if you should put her there. Either way, you are getting her to her bed. Give your little one a snuggle, kiss her, say goodnight, and walk out of her room.

The last 0.219 miles of a marathon is when you are searching your mind to figure out how you are going to finish the race. Your child is doing the same. But her thoughts are a bit different. She is thinking, "How am I going to postpone this bedtime routine?" Get on your work boots, folks, and learn to say, "I'm sorry ..."

- "I'm sorry, you cannot have a glass of water."
- "I'm sorry, reading is over."
- "I'm sorry you are hungry; I will be serving a tasty breakfast in the morning." Do not say, "You should have eaten your dinner when I told you too"; only discuss breakfast.
- "I'm sorry you want another hug; it's time for bed."
- "I'm sorry you want six more stuffed animals in your bed; ten is enough."

You get the point. The answer is no. The race is over. It's bedtime. And, most importantly, it's time for you to have a moment to yourself. So be polite; repeat, repeat, repeat; and get your children to bed. And don't hop in bed with your kids for a snuggle—hop in bed with your partner for a snuggle!

Getting Your Kid a Phone

Parents, don't be so afraid of the phone. Think of the phone as the best little piece of discipline and responsibility. Your child having a phone makes your life easier. It's great when you can send your child a text to say you will be five minutes late. Or your kid can send you a text and say, "I forgot my lunch," and you can write back, "I'm sorry, I don't have time to bring it to you." The phone is a great thing. You don't have to get a smartphone, so don't worry about all the games and the Internet. Just get your kid a phone that texts and calls a few numbers—a starter phone. And then enjoy the benefits.

The phone will teach your child responsibility because she will need to keep track of it. If she loses it then she needs to earn the money to buy another one. If she is rude to you on or off the phone, take the phone. Think of the phone as your child's first car. She learns responsibility very quickly. She also can use that wonderful little device to get some work done for you.

1. Have your child call the plumber and set up an appointment to fix a broken pipe.
2. Have him call the mail service to put a hold on your mail prior to a vacation.
3. Have her call and schedule her next dentist's appointment.
4. Have him call and refill prescriptions from the pharmacy.
5. Have her call and set up her sleepovers (she should be used to this because she has been doing it from your phone for years).

The list goes on and on. And, yes, your child could do all of this on your phone, but how cool is it if she gets to use her own phone? Very cool for her, and even cooler for you.

Homework

Your children's homework came home with them: it is their homework, not yours. It is not for you to sit down next to your children as they complete each sentence, do every math problem, or color every picture. This is not how it works in your child's classroom. The teachers are there to answer questions and teach, but not to hover over your children and correct every mistake and say, "Are you sure?" when they write something down wrong.

SIDE NOTE

Teddy was doing his homework after school on a Friday. He was having trouble with syllables. I knew he was; I could see the look on his face from the kitchen. I didn't offer to help him. Yes, I wanted to. But it's his work. I waited until he politely asked me for help. When he did, we stepped away from his homework and I gave him a quick syllables lesson. He seemed to understand what I was saying and went back to his homework. As he was finishing up his homework, I glanced at it, and from what I could tell, he got all the syllable work wrong. Obviously, the syllable lesson at school didn't hit a homerun with Teddy, and I wanted the teacher to know it. The only way she was going to figure that out was if he returned his homework with the information he knew.

Of course, I love teaching our children new things. But I'm not a schoolteacher and we don't homeschool. So I gave

Teddy the best lesson on syllables I could. It didn't click, so I didn't try again. I knew we would both end up frustrated. And we all know when something gets frustrating—especially when you are first learning it—the magic of the new lesson or experience can sometimes get lost. Teddy finished up his homework and was very happy. I let him pack up his work in his school bag and finish up his weekend. Monday he and his teacher would discover he didn't understand syllables. Maybe he wasn't the only one and the lesson needed to be retaught to the entire class. I never looked into it or heard about any problems.

For younger children just starting out in the world of homework, you need to help them get started. In our family, homework is *always* done the minute we walk in the door from school. This may not work for your family, but for ours, it does. The reason we like it is because right after school, the children are still in "school mode," and once their homework is complete, they have the rest of the evening and weekends free.

Our homework plan may not work for your family. Often, afterschool activities get in the way. I keep a set of pens and pencils in my car for children who need to finish their homework while another child is doing an afterschool activity, or for between activities. Figure out what works for your family. Does your child need a snack when you walk in the door? Could you save time and bring a snack to eat right after school? Does your child need 30 minutes to unwind? If so, set a timer. Does your child want to have a friend over? Let them, but have the kids work on homework first. I know this may sound like a bad idea, but your child has the friends around them all day long in school, and they are learning tons. There is no reason the same can't happen at home. If your children have a lot of homework, set a timer and have them work on it in 15-minute increments: 15 minutes of work, 10 minutes of play. This worked great for Ian when he was younger. Eventually, he just gave up on the timer and finished his homework so he could ~~go play~~ without any interruptions. Whatever program you pick, be kind to your children while they adjust to having homework in their life.

Find a place in your house where your children will succeed at doing homework, where they have all the supplies they need. Have your children start their homework at the preselected time. Do not sit with your children while they do their homework. Don't you dare pull up a chair. Tell them to complete what they can do, and skip what they cannot. Once your children complete their homework, tell them to go back through it to see if they can answer any questions they skipped. If a child cannot answer a question, have her call a friend to ask for help. Or, if she can, email the teacher. If that's not possible, ask her to tell you what she knows from the lesson in class. And if she still doesn't come up with the right answer, it's okay for her to go to school with the wrong one. The teacher will most likely pull her aside and teach it to her. Maybe a few other kids got the same answer wrong and the teacher will decide to give the lesson over again.

Do everything you can to not hover over your children's homework. The grades they get now are an example of what they will get in the future. Young children are eager to learn; keep them eager as they feel the successes of completing their own work. Let them and their teachers see what they do and do not know.

You know those big art projects that look like the parents did them? Homework is *no* different. Don't do your kids' art projects, drawings, book reports, or dioramas; don't do any of it.

If you sit there and hover over your children as they complete their homework, and if you are 100% available to answer every question that pops into their heads, why would your they ever try to figure out the answers for themselves? They don't need to, because you are sitting right there spoon-feeding them the answers, and their brains can just keep on sleeping. Our brains *need* exercise, and thinking is our brains' exercise. Let your children's brains get exercise. Step away, folks, step away. These years are the years where your children get to (and have to) learn. If your kiddos don't figure out how to problem solve now, how will college or the real world or whatever they pursue work out for them? Don't screw them up by hovering over their homework. If they figure it out for themselves now, they will be able to figure it out when it really counts. Let your children teach themselves to learn. They cannot do this with you hovering over them.

Issues at School

Children start school as early as age two—sooner if you include daycare. Teach your children to manage their own issues at school. Teach them to be their own voices. Most teachers are fabulous at talking to kids. The next time your little one or older child has an issue at school, discuss it with him at home. Ask a lot of open-ended questions; get your child thinking. You and your child may decide it's not worth discussing, or you may decide on an email to the teacher from your child. Whatever you come up with, you will be empowering your child to be responsible for his own issues; you will be teaching him to solve life's little challenges himself.

We started long ago with having Ian manage his own issues at school. We taught him that if he didn't like a grade he got to go discuss it with the teacher. We supported him. We talked him through how we thought it might go. Before one of Ian's physics exams, he asked one of his teachers if he could leave class early to study for his next class. On his way to study, he ran into his physics teacher in the hall. He asked the teacher if he would study with him and the teacher said yes. Ian got a lot of questions answered in that study session with the teacher. Before this, I know Ian would never have asked a teacher for assistance before an exam, or to leave a class early, but he did both. We know he is figuring out how to navigate his life so it works for him. And he is succeeding every step of the way.

One afternoon, Teddy was showing me his schoolwork. He showed me his science report. He got an 8 out of 10. He was not happy with his grade. I told him he should ask the teacher why. I could already see why, but I wasn't the teacher, and this was a perfect opportunity for Teddy to speak up. So he got out a Post-it note and wrote the teacher a note, posted it to the homework, and turned it back in. He got his answer the next day. He hadn't answered one of the questions correctly. He still wasn't happy about his grade, but he was proud his teacher responded to his note.

Say It Once; Repeat ONLY if Needed

I have talked a little bit about my voice and how I get tired of hearing it. I do, and so do my children, and so does my husband. We would all be such bigger, better people if we talked less and listened more. You know the people you meet who talk and talk and talk, and you can't get a word in? You try to listen, but what they are saying is so boring. Your kids feel the same way when you start in about something—especially when you are nagging. So when it comes to our children and discipline, we try to only say it once—or don't say anything and let natural consequences do their work.

Before you open your mouth to ask your child to do something or to discipline them or to say anything negative, pause and see if you really need to speak. If you do, then figure out how you are going to say it only once and in as few words as possible. If needed, repeat your words, but only if you need to.

SIDE NOTE

When Teddy was four, he had some traits of a 90-year-old. When I would say it's time to get ready to go (which I say 15 minutes before it's actually time to leave), my kids know they need to get ready ASAP. Harvey grabs his Crocs and runs around screaming, "CROCS!" waiting for someone to put them on. Murphy goes on autopilot and gets ready. Ian, obviously, has mastered this program.

The other morning, Teddy pulled this ... I gave the 15-minute warning. Teddy got his shoes and then took a minute or two telling Murphy how great she looked, giving us 13 minutes to get in the car. Then Teddy moved on to Harvey (while he was holding his shoes, but no socks) and discussed with him what jacket he was going to wear, while Harvey was screaming at him, "Crocs, Crocs, Crocs!"

The countdown to get in the car was 10 minutes. Yes, they were all cute and funny, but I needed to leave. I looked at Teddy, trying to follow my rule of not asking him to put his shoes on, and I squinted my eyes, thinking he would know I just wanted him to put his fucking shoes on—but no. He said, "Mama, I love your hair today!" We were seven minutes in and Murphy was ready and waiting at the door; Harvey had screamed his last "Croc" because I jammed them on his feet. Five minutes to go. I had my coat on, my purse on, and my shoes on, and I unlocked the car. Three minutes. Teddy was looking out the window telling me about the neighbor walking his dog and that it looked like he had gotten a new leash. One minute. I could barely hear Teddy jabbering because I was buckling Murphy and Harvey in the car. And Teddy looked at us, looked at his bare feet, and said, "I don't have any socks."

Here's the thing, if I nagged at Teddy the entire time, begging, asking, pleading with him to put his shoes on—or worse, if I had put his shoes on for him—the whole situation would have gone from positive to negative. My nagging would make me pissed that Teddy wasn't hustling. Teddy wouldn't be learning time management; Teddy wouldn't be learning that when he comes downstairs he needs to bring his socks. Yes, I get super-irritated with him wandering around chitchatting with everyone, observing the world, etc., etc. ... but there is no harm in it, and really, it is pretty beautiful and amazing to hear all these funny things coming out of a four-year-old. So I have learned to just keep my mouth shut and let the mornings unfold as they will. I just make sure I am sitting in the car when I need to be so I can start pulling out of the driveway. And that day when Teddy finally got in the car holding his shoes and socks, he said to me, "I should have gotten my stuff on inside." Trust me, moms and dads, their brains work. It all sinks in, so just say it once and let the natural consequences occur, because they will *learn*.

SIDE NOTE

One weekend I was alone with Wiggy. She asked for a snack plate for breakfast. I put some dried fruit, fresh fruit, cheese, and crackers on a plate and set it in front of her at the table. Instead of saying "thank you," she complained about the fruit and the crackers. Before she could finish her rant, I walked over, took the plate, and put all the food away. She wasn't surprised. She said she wanted breakfast; I said (very politely), "I'm sorry." She didn't ask why she didn't get breakfast. She knew. I didn't need to go on some rant about how rude she was to me. What's the point? I would just get more pissed listening to her argue about every word out of my mouth. Now if she had asked why she didn't get breakfast, I would tell her very simply because she complained about the food I served her rather than saying "thank you."

Here are some ways to just say things once and let life unfold as it will:

- Mealtime. Sit down at the table and tell everyone what you served them for food. If you need to, remind everyone of the rules at the table and the consequences. Then stick to your guns. One kid steps out of line, he is done; you don't need to say a word except to tell him to clear his plate and when the next meal will be served. Do not say anything else. Ignore the screams and cries.

• This works for husbands too! If I write a story about David, he will kill me, but I'll do it anyway. The other day, I asked him to take the laundry up (I had hurt my back, so I wasn't supposed to lift anything). Anyway, he said, "Sure, in a bit." I wanted to get my stuff done, so I just took the basket up myself. He saw me bringing the empty basket downstairs and said, "I would have done that." I said, "It's okay, it's done." I wasn't pissed, I didn't nag. I was happy I got my stuff done before we went out. Just say it once and let it go.

Just say what you need to say once. Don't nag, don't bitch; words are powerful, and the fewer you use, the stronger your case. Don't be that annoying person who talks too much.

Thank You

When the opportunity presents itself, say "thank you" to your children and partner. Don't go overboard here. Don't thank your kid for walking in the door or taking a sip of milk; keep it reasonable. Thank your children for completing the bedtime routine in a speedy fashion, for sitting at the meal table nicely; thank your children for being polite to your guests. And don't forget to thank your partner. I know, sometimes we just don't want to; *I get it*. But just suck it up and thank your partner.

Money

There are many schools of thoughts here. Should you give your child an allowance for doing chores around the house? Some say "no" because children should contribute to the household and not require payment. Others say "yes" because one should be paid for his work. I say, pay your children an allowance. Kids need money and you don't want to be a bank machine every time your child needs lunch money, new cleats, or cash for movie tickets. So pay your kids. Act just like an employment agency. Pay your kids on the same day of every week. And require them to help around the house. In our house, I keep it very simple. The children have daily things they need to do. Get themselves ready in the morning, clear their dishes from the table, be polite, make their lunches, make their beds, clean their rooms, and clean up after themselves. In addition to that, the kids owe me two hours of their time on the weekends to get work done around the house. I keep a list of tasks I need done, and it's the kids' job to complete those tasks for me. We all chat on Friday about when a good time is for them to give me their two hours. Tasks on the weekend include raking leaves, cleaning out basement window wells, vacuuming cars, cleaning light fixtures, changing light bulbs, cleaning out the pantry, cleaning out the fridge, cleaning bathrooms; I have even had them changing all the toilet seats in the house, changing batteries in broken toys, organizing the garage, etc. The chore list does two things. One, it checks a bunch of tasks off my list. Two, our kids learn so many skills, about working, about completing a job, and the list goes on and on.

I remember the first weekend after we started paying Ian an allowance, he asked for money to walk to Starbucks for breakfast. I smiled and said, "You have your own money." He said, "I don't want to use my own money for breakfast." I said, "Then you can have breakfast for free here." He ate at home. Lots of learning happening. Ian was happy to spend my money for breakfast, but when he had some skin in the game and his breakfast expenses came out of his own wallet, the game changed.

SIDE NOTE

During Ian's freshman year in high school we decided to give him a lump sum of money per semester for all of his spending needs. He would be off to college in four years and we wanted to give him more responsibility. The money was to pay for school supplies, soccer gear, school lunch, everything. The day before school started, I gave him his money. He put some of the money on his student account; he could buy lunch, snacks, and other supplies with that. A few weeks into school, I said, "Why do you always make your lunch? You have plenty of money to buy lunch at school." He said his friend had $100 on his account and it was gone in the first month from buying lunches and snacks at school; he said he couldn't afford not to pack his lunch!

How else would he have learned that lesson? Not by us giving him lunch money every day, that's for sure.

ANOTHER SIDE NOTE

Teddy wears uniforms to school. Occasionally, the kids can pay $2 for various fundraisers and they can wear their street clothes; it's called free dress. Teddy was five and in kindergarten for his first free dress. He asked for $2 so he could wear his regular clothes. I told him he could dig into his piggy bank for $2 and wear whatever he wanted to school, or he could wear his uniform for free. He wore his uniform.

There are little ways everywhere to teach your kids about money. So start paying your kids, and let them spend their money as they wish. They will quickly learn it doesn't last forever.

Clothing

Keeping track of children's clothing—what size they are, what they have grown into or out of, who needs what, who lost what, what can be passed to the next child or neighbor, what is worn out—could truly be a job all its own. For our children, I buy only what we need. I don't go to Target for diapers and walk out with a few new pieces of clothing for the kids. I know, I know, the kids' clothes are so cute. I get it.

I learned this lesson long ago. Ian needed a new winter coat, so I went to our local ski shop and bought him the cutest down jacket. I was so excited to see this little five-year-old in a puffy jacket. He wouldn't wear the jacket; he didn't like the color, he didn't like the puffiness of it. I was bummed and kinda pissed. Here I had taken my time to go to the store, pick out something I liked, and basically presented him with a gift, and it wasn't even a holiday. He wasn't having it. I learned so much from that jacket. Never again was I going to buy a kid clothing without his approval, *unless* I was willing to accept the rejection and return the item.

Children do not need a lot of clothing. When our children were babies, I would only buy them three to four outfits per size range. I do a lot of laundry and it just seemed easier to have fewer decisions when I was dressing them. At about age 1 ½ to 2 years, children start wanting to make their clothing choices.

Like I said, clothing is only purchased in our family on a "needs" basis. About twice a year, we go through the kids' clothes. This means each of the kids and I go through every single piece of clothing in each of their closets—including jackets, hats, and shoes. My first question is, "Do you wear this?" If the answer is "no," the clothing is moved to our hand-me-down closet. If the answer is yes, then I ask, "Does it fit?" If it fits, we keep it; if not, it goes to the hand-me-down closet. After that, we check our hand-me-down closet to replenish. If we can't find what we need there, we hop online and our children pick out only what they need. It's easy and our children's dressers are not overflowing. Plus, I am teaching our children to manage their own clothing. And, hopefully, that they do not need tons of clothing to live.

Here's a little more detail about how the children manage their clothing:

- Each child picks out his clothes for the day. I don't pick out his clothes with him in the morning or the night before. Sometimes I may suggest the kids dress warm because it's cold out or that they might not want to wear flip-flops because it's raining. Sometimes they take my suggestions and sometimes they don't. As they have gotten older, they have asked me to check the weather before they pick out their clothing for the day. Getting dressed in our home has always been this simple, and it's because I have never made a huge deal about it. I let them wear what they want. If their schools have clothing rules, then they need to follow those rules. If they choose not to, I let the school deal with it.

- Our children get dressed and (for the most part) politely ask for help if they need it. And if they don't ask politely, I happily ignore them until I hear "please." I am not about to help a kid who is rudely asking for help. The kids pick out their shoes and put on their socks and shoes and again ask for help if they need it. I don't intervene in the shoe department. My kids have learned that splashing in puddles in boots is better than in Crocs. And playing soccer in tennis shoes is faster than in cowboy boots. I have not taught them that through intervention; they have learned that on their own. And, most importantly, our children do not have a lot of shoes. Our boys each have one pair of shoes. Wiggy has a few more because she has gotten hand-me-downs from friends.

- There are several areas in the clothing department where I draw the line: cleanliness, formal events, underwear, and illness.

  - Our children's clothes are cleaned daily. I don't always know where my children have been all day. I don't know if they have chosen to sit on the floor in the school bathroom or if they spilled orange juice all over their jeans or if they got snuggling with a friend who had the flu. Instead of playing the guessing game, all clothes go in the dirty laundry at the end of the day. Our children understand they may not be able to wear a cherished item because it's in the wash. I do not kill myself to get the favorite superman shirt washed and dried every night. It's a piece of clothing and it will be available to wear when the laundry gets done, on my time.

- Like all families, we have nice events we go to from time to time, and the kids need to dress accordingly. I tell them we have a nice event and to please pick out some nice clothing to wear. They pick out what they think is "nice" and I may do a bit of editing. They aren't always excited for the changes I make, but they are more excited to head to an event, so they ignore the changes or choose not to fight them.

- Our children wear underwear. No exceptions. There is *no* discussion. None, zero, zilch. Your children should wear underwear. Don't let your children tell you it's uncomfortable. It's okay if your children are uncomfortable at times; they will survive. And all you need to say to your child is, "I'm sorry your underwear isn't comfortable. Try them out today and let me know how they feel at the end of the day." Chances are you won't hear another word about it—and if you don't, *do not ask about it*. If after a few days your little one is still complaining about their underwear, they may need a different fit. Just have your kids wear underwear!

• When our children are sick I assist in their clothing choices. That's if they must leave the house. I don't send sick children to school and I hope you don't either.

SIDE NOTE

I had a playdate a few years ago and a friend's daughter came over. The kids were playing and running and having a blast. Then they were reading on the couch, and all of a sudden, the friend's dress popped up, and no panties. I said to the mom, "Your daughter is missing her panties." She said, "No, I can't get her to wear them." I was horrified, disgusted, and disturbed. Here's the deal: you tell your kids they can't leave for a playdate until they have panties on. And you bring a couple of extra pairs for the kid who continues to take off her panties. Be in charge, parents.

• Dressing for cold weather: I guide the kids on how to dress in cold weather, but I do not force them to wear a bunch of clothes. I want them to learn how to dress. Now, if someone has a cold, they know I am going to insist they dress a little warmer. Or if we are headed outdoors for an extended period of time, I tell them to bring this and that because we are going hiking or whatever. But for the day-to-day stuff, they pick. We don't live in an extreme climate here in Portland, Oregon. Don't fight this battle with your kids if it is not a life or death situation, as it is in some places. It is not worth the battle. Let them go to school without a coat. Again, less talking, moms, dads, and caregivers—that means more learning for kids. Your child may miss recess because he doesn't have the appropriate clothing, or he may be forced to wear something from the lost and found—but guess who will decide to bring a coat next time? Often, when we are outside and it's 35 degrees out, one of our children will ask to take his coat off. I say, sure, go for it. Yes, other parents stare. My kid takes his coat off, runs around for one minute, and is back asking to put the coat back on. And all I had to say to my kid was "sure." No nagging, no argument, nothing. I just let life do the teaching. The other thing is that you have no idea how your child's body is feeling. Let your children be in charge of listening to how their bodies are feeling. Two of our boys wear shorts and no jackets to school every day. Kids are little heaters.

SIDE NOTE

Last year Teddy's teachers asked me if we could please dress Teddy in pants because it was around 30 degrees during the day. Teddy always wears shorts. So the next day as Teddy was getting dressed for school, I reminded him his teachers wanted him to wear pants. Teddy put on pants. He went to school, and all was good. After school I picked Teddy up and his teachers apologized. They said Teddy was red in the face all day because he was so hot from the pants. They never asked him to wear pants again. Kids know; they know how to dress their bodies. And if they don't, let them learn, and stay out of it.

SIDE NOTE

I once saw a kid in fleece pajamas on a 90-degree day. I said, "Wow, that kid must be hot." The parent said, "Yeah, he won't take it off." I don't know about you, but I am a lot stronger than all four of our children. I let my kids have a lot of freedoms in their closets, but I will not let them wear the same thing over and over. I wash their clothes after they wear them once. My children understand their clothes are washed at the end of each day. And, sometimes, The Kelleher Basement Laundromat does not have a 12-hour wash and dry policy. It might take a day or two to get something back. They are okay with that. They can wait. Have you heard of *The Marshmallow Test*? Read it.

I'm Sorry

We do not *ever* ask our children to say "I'm sorry." Ever.

SIDE NOTE

A month or so ago, we walked to dinner with some friends, with their one child and three of ours. Their child hit Teddy hard and he cried; their child knew he had done something wrong. I asked Teddy if he was okay, I told him I was sorry he got hit, and I was ready to continue our walk to dinner. But the little guy's parents (the child who hit our child) felt horrible. And they spent 10 to 15 minutes making us all wait while they tried to force their son to say "sorry" to our child. Seriously, we all stood there uncomfortably on the sidewalk while they begged, pleaded, and bribed their child to say it. The whole lesson about whether or not you should hit someone was lost. The fact that this kid hit our kid was gone with the wind. Instead, these parents had a battle with their child's vocal cords.

How would I have handled the above situation? Every time a kid hits another kid, it's always a bummer, but each situation is different. The bottom line is that I want my child to understand we do not hit. In this circumstance, I would have apologized to the little boy and the parents; modeling great behavior is the best and strongest form of parenting. And then I would have asked the little boy if he was okay. And, lastly, I would have taken my little offender off to the side away from everyone and told everyone else to keep walking to dinner (so no one had to wait) and had my little guy have a seat by himself on the sidewalk until he was "ready." (I put "ready" in quotations because you will learn about this later.) Having my child sit there watching everyone walk away to dinner is the start of the punishment. Then I would ask my little offender to tell me why he hit, and why it's wrong, and then away we would go to dinner. That would be the end of the discipline. No one would be waiting for me to do a full court press punishment.

Saying "I'm sorry" is *awesome*! But if you don't mean it, and someone has either asked you to say it or you are saying it to get out of the situation you are in, someone, somewhere went wrong with you long ago. And if you are forcing your children to say "I'm sorry" for something they have done, the lesson is lost. Very lost: it's gone forever. The only thing you are teaching your children is that "I'm sorry" is the "Get Out of Jail Free" card for bad behavior, and they don't have to feel a thing or change future behaviors. So, instead, focus on the bad action your child did. Show her that someone is crying because she hit him. Or someone's feelings are hurt because he got left out. Show your child the results of her poor behavior or decisions. You don't have to make a major Broadway production; just point it out and move on. This incident is most likely a tiny blip in life.

I could look this up, but since I have been through all the age groups up to teens, I can pretty confidently say kids don't really understand the true meaning of connecting "I'm sorry" with emotions until about age six, seven, or maybe even eight. And that's if they are lucky, and their parents, teachers, and friends have let them learn the true meaning of it and didn't force them to say it.

So next time your kid smacks another kid, or steals a toy, or yells at you, or whatever, punish the behavior. Don't try to use a Roto-Rooter to get two simple words out of your child.

Pause

One important piece of ammunition to have in your arsenal of parenting is "the pause." Before you snap, before you discipline, before you scream at your kid, before you take a toy away, before you grab a kid a little roughly (trust me, we have all done it), before you lose it, *pause*. Just pause, take a deep breath and get calm. Fill your body with oxygen and remember the age of your little one. Then and only then should you deliver whatever you were going to deliver to your little one. You will speak clearer, you will think clearer, and you won't get as mad, which means you probably won't raise your voice. Remember, you are the one teaching your child to communicate. Do a good job.

The pause also helps you out of those jams when you aren't sure how to respond. Take a moment of silence. Your kids know when they misbehave. The pause gives you a moment to collect yourself, get calm, and get a plan. The pause will also allow your children a moment to think about what they have done wrong. And when your kids get older and do the unthinkable (sneak out, get caught drinking, take the car without asking, whatever), you don't have to get mad at them right away. Pause, get calm, and get a plan. Your punishment will be so much clearer and well-thought-out if it's delivered when you are calm.

While you are pausing, think about "the why"—*why* what your child did was wrong. Get specific in your head and then get very specific about how you want to handle it. Let's say Wiggy takes a marker out of Harvey's hand while he is coloring. It's simple: Wiggy is done coloring. But this may have been the last straw for me. I may be so irritated because everyone has been acting up all morning and I have PMS … bad combination. Anyway, I could easily go off the handle on Wiggy for simply taking a marker. But if I pause, get calm, and think about what kind of punishment is really necessary, I am so much happier with the outcome. And I feel so much better as a parent. And Wiggy doesn't feel like it's the end of the world for taking a marker. In this situation, I wouldn't need to say a word—I can simply remove Wiggy from the coloring and she can find something else to do. If our children are taking markers away from other children without asking, they don't get to continue coloring.

SIDE NOTE

Pause ... The other day, Harvey swung his "baby" at Teddy very hard and hit him. David saw what happened and was really mad. We all sat in silence for what seemed like forever as David stood there staring at Harvey. David just looked at Harvey and said nothing. He did it: he did the pause. I walked in and David told me what happened. I picked up Harvey, took his baby, put him straight to bed (it was close to bedtime), told him I loved him, and closed his door. There was no need for David or me to say a word. Teddy was crying, so Harvey knew he had hurt Teddy. I took Harvey's baby because it isn't supposed to be a weapon. We didn't even need to figure out a punishment; in that case, we used no words—the pause was enough. If you do need to say something to your child, use the pause to calm yourself down and then figure out exactly what your child did wrong and how you would like to handle the situation. When I carried Harvey away to bed, he was kicking and screaming; the punishment was complete. He was removed from the fun and put to bed and he knew why.

Be a Polite Parent and Discipline with Manners and Kindness

I am not the most well-mannered person in the world by a long, long shot. However, I do know my manners. This tip is simple: *always* be polite to your children and they will be polite to you and everyone around them, most of the time. If every single word out of your mouth is politely and lovingly spoken to your child, guess what you will get in return? A child who speaks politely. Your children learn how to speak, tone of voice, and words to use from you and their other caregivers. So if you are using rude words or an angry tone, or if you are yelling at your children, you are going to get the same from them. But if you say "please" and "thank you" to your children, discipline them with kind words, and use a gentler tone, you will hear the same from them. Punishments do not need to be delivered with yelling and anger. You can deliver a brutal punishment to your children with kind words. Anger and screaming at your children will not deliver a better, stronger message. Instead, it's a production or a play, if you will, for your children to see exactly how to behave rudely, and you are the starring character.

Just because you are being kind to your children while you are banning them from sleepovers for the weekend doesn't mean they will be polite back at that moment. They are going to be pissed, and that's okay. Remind yourself that you are setting a long, solid foundation of respect for one another. Yes, you rule the roost, but that does not mean you need to rule it rudely.

If you speak in a kinder tone when you are chatting with your kids or disciplining them, there will be a shift in your home, I promise. The most amazing thing I have noticed for myself about raising our kids with manners is that I have kids who are learning manners, which is great. But the other thing for me is that when I discipline with manners, I don't get as fired up or irritated or worked up over the situation. Most of the time, I stay pretty calm—I am very clear with my words, and the situation does not tend to spiral out of control. The effect is that the kids don't seem to spiral out of control either. So be polite.

Then next time you need to scold your children for *whatever*, do it politely. Just because you are mad doesn't mean you need to use a mean voice. No need to scare children or be mean. Just correct their behavior with a nice, quiet voice and move on. Now, let's be honest here, sometimes you will lose your temper. Get over it. It happens. Think about what you can do so you don't lose your temper next time. Would the pause help you in this situation? How about a breath of fresh air, or a shot of tequila? What's the trick for you? It will take time to figure this out, but it's worth it.

Deliver Your Punishment in 20 Words or Less

Deliver your child's punishment in 20 words. That's it. Say more than 20 words, and you will lose your child's attention. You will also go into shaming your child and putting him down. So slim it down to 20 words. The only way you can do this is to pause and get calm. Trust me, you can do this. Here are some examples:

- Your child took your car without asking. You say, "I'm sorry you can't use the car for two weeks." 10 words.
- Your child threw food at the table. You say, "I'm sorry, your dinner is over. Please clear your place." 10 words. (Notice how I say "please" and "I'm sorry" even while I'm punishing. I'm modeling good manners, even when I'm pissed off.)
- Keep in simple, folks.

Speak Slowly

While you are punishing your child, speak slowly. Yep, that's it, just slow it down. You will not get that mean tone of voice (the one you inherit when you become a parent). You also can't yell or scream as easily if you are talking slowly. So *slow it down*.

Punishment and Natural Consequences

Punishments in our house are very simple. It can go one of two ways: one, we don't have to say a word because some sort of natural consequences are doing the work for us. Or, two, we say as few words as possible to get our point across and let the offender do most of the talking. Here are some examples:

- A child spills his milk. He most likely spills it because he is learning how to balance his milk in a "big boy" cup and isn't totally paying attention. There is no need for me to say anything. I may offer to grab him a paper towel so he can clean it up or even offer to help him clean it up. But that's it, folks. Nobody wants to spill their milk. That's it, that's the punishment: the spilled milk.

- Or a child spills her milk because she is screwing around at the dinner table. Now it's time for me to talk. I keep it simple, "Your dinner is over. Please clear your plate and clean up your area." I ignore the screaming and crying and complaining. I do not carry on with the punishment. All her screaming and crying means the punishment is happening. My thirteen words did the trick. That's the punishment.

- I tell a child to tidy up her room and she refuses. When it's time to do our next activity, I say, "I'm sorry, you can't start the art project until your room is clean." The problem is not mine; it isn't my fault the child can't start the activity. She made the choice to not clean her room earlier. She screams and cries as she heads up to her room to clean it up. Punishment complete. When your children are screaming and crying, you have accomplished their punishment. You have struck a nerve with them.

- A child won't eat his dinner. It's not your problem; say nothing. He will be punishing himself when he is hungry later and the kitchen is closed.

- Someone speaks rudely to me on the phone. I politely tell him to come home promptly and that I will keep track of his phone for a couple of days.
- One of our children pushes another one down. I give the child crying on the ground tons of love, and tell the other kid to "have a seat."

You get the point. Punishments don't need to be that big of a deal and they need to fit the crime. When you use natural consequences as punishments, you don't need to address the situation too much because the consequences do that for you. This takes time to learn; slow your punishments down, you will get it.

Have a Seat

Besides loving our children and providing them with the basic needs, this is the best parenting thing we have done in our family. If natural consequences don't work and we need to act, we tell our kids to "have a seat." And when our children are done sitting there, they say, "I'm ready." It's that simple—so simple we can discipline our children anywhere. I've been at birthday parties and been able to discipline one of our children while barely missing a conversation. From across the schoolyard, I can tell one of our kids to "have a seat." They either drop where they are or come over to me and have seat.

This is not a timeout. I don't like the word "timeout." Why? I don't know; probably because I have heard so many parents say, "I'm going to give you a timeout," or, "Do you need a timeout?" And if you are talking about the timeout, you should have already given the timeout. I also don't like timeouts because it requires the little felon to sit there for an unknown period of time, set by the parent. I think the unknown is just adding insult to injury. And more importantly, it requires whoever is disciplining to set a timer; that's too much work. Imagine if you had to wait in line for an unknown period of time? You rarely do. If you are waiting on hold on the phone, the recording tells you how many minutes you will be waiting or that you are the tenth caller, or if you are waiting in an actual line, you can see how many people are ahead of you. Imagine if, in all these cases, you had no idea how long you would be waiting? It would be super frustrating. Same thing with timeouts, your kids have no idea how long they will be sitting there. So the whole time they are sitting there, they are thinking about how much longer they will be there, not why they are sitting there. The way we do it (have a seat) doesn't require a timer, talking, or negotiating; all we need is a naughty child.

Telling our children to "have a seat" gives our little offenders a chance to calm down and gather their thoughts. It also gives us a chance to calm down and think about how we want to handle the situation. It also pulls the children out of the situation they are in; it defuses the situation. Our children know that when they are done sitting on the stair they need to come to one of us and explain what they have done wrong and why it's wrong. They can get off the stair by simply saying, "I'm ready." They come over to us and they have our undivided attention to talk. If they decide not to talk, then we will tell them what they did wrong and how they could have handled the situation differently.

Lots and lots and lots of screaming meltdowns have been had on our stairs. But those are not my problem. I have learned to ignore the screams because I know the screams mean the punishment is happening. Even Ian is told to "have a seat" when our conversations with him aren't going well. And it gives him and us a chance to cool down.

The first time I used the stair, Teddy was two. He would not sit politely at the dinner table. I told him he could not sit at the table and behave this way, I put him on the stair, and I told him to tell me when he was "ready" to come back to the table and sit politely. He kicked and cried and screamed on the stair and we had to listen to it. I was just happy he wasn't sitting next to me anymore having his tantrum. Eventually, he calmed down and said he was ready. He came back to the table and acted up again. I said the same thing and put him back on the stair. Same thing, he kicked, screamed, cried, and then said he was ready. Eventually, he understood he had to politely sit at the table. Sometimes I put the same child on the stair 20 times before lunch and it gets exhausting. But it works.

- It works because there is always a place to have a seat. It doesn't have to be a stair. It can be a bench, the ground, a corner of a room, anywhere. We don't need a naughty mat or timeout chair.
- It works because I don't have to go into an exhausting tirade with my children; they know that if they are sent to the stair they have done something wrong.
- It works because I don't have to say anything besides "have a seat."
- It works because it gives my children an opportunity to be in charge of their punishments.
- It works because I don't have to manage a "timeout" clock; my kids just tell me when they are ready to discuss the issue at hand.

- It works because when you send your child away from a toy, sibling, or bad situation, you break up the problem.
- It works because when I send children to the stair, they get a moment to calm down.
- It works because it is so easy to tell your child to have a seat politely, no matter how pissed off you are.

This little discipline tool can be tough to get rolling in your house. But once you get on board, you can discipline your child at a party, and no one will even know. I have gone up to my children at the park and whispered, "Have a seat." Then I go back to chatting with my friends, and when the children are ready, they come over, tell me what they have done wrong, and they are back to playing in no time. I don't even have to bat an eyelash. I don't have to say more than three words. I don't scream. And my children don't get shamed because I tell them they are in trouble in front of anyone.

The first few times you put a kid on the stair, she is going to get up. Just pick her up, put her back on the stair, and tell her she can get up when she is ready. Those are the only words you say to her. Do not tell her why she is there. Do not tell her to stay. Do not say anything except, "You can get up when you are ready." And repeat and repeat and repeat. Your children will eventually understand; just stick with the program.

Let Them Tell You ... If They Will

This is a follow-up to "have a seat." This is a tricky one. Anytime our kids have done something wrong, I give them one chance, and one chance only, to tell me what they did wrong and why they did it. If they don't start talking, then I tell them what they did wrong and how they can do things differently next time. Your children must feel safe enough with you to tell you what they did wrong. They have to know that you aren't going to flip out on them. Most kids won't tell the truth or tell you what they did wrong. I'm the same; when I get pulled over for speeding, I never say, "Yes, officer, I knew I was doing 40 in a 20 mph zone." Nope, I play stupid. Your kid will do the same. So give your kid one shot to tell you the truth, and if he decides not to, don't quickly jump down his throat for not telling you. Instead, stay on course with the original offense and tell him what he did wrong. Don't yell at your children, don't shame them, just keep it simple and say you cannot write on the living room walls with a Sharpie because that's not how we treat our home. Get out the Magic Eraser and have your child start cleaning. End of story. Also, put all the Sharpies in a better spot and let it go, folks.

Now, if you have a kid who will tell you the truth right off the bat, the same rules apply: *do not flip out on your kid*. Keep the vibe calm and safe (no yelling). Teach your children they will not get throttled for telling you what they did wrong. They don't need to get praised for it either—but if you keep the vibe good, your children will not be afraid to come to you with issues in their lives. Remember, you have to pave the way for them to feel this way.

A couple of things to keep in mind: my kids are always shocked about how much of the story I do know. They cannot believe that from my bedroom putting away laundry I heard Harvey scream at the dog and Murphy kick him in the shin for doing it while they were outside in the yard. I always remind them I know everything and can hear everything. And if I don't know the whole story, I will *always* figure it out.

This is a long play. You want your children to talk to you and feel comfortable talking to you. You want open lines of communication. You want your kids to tell you what is really going on their lives. A great way to do this is to keep the vibe and response calm and cool, no matter what your kids are telling you. You want them to keep talking, and they will if you let them. Start this now so when your kiddos are teens and have some real issues you are the one they turn to. This is also a great opportunity to teach your children how to talk during stressful situations. So be kind and cool and calm as your kiddo tells you they made a dog poop brownie for their sister and she ate it.

Shame

I have seen a counselor for a number of years. I enjoy it. It's my 60 minutes of undivided attention. I used to go in there every week and talk about my life, good and bad. Today I see her every couple of months if something big in our life rears its head or if I just need a tune-up. I learned and am still learning so much from her. One of her biggest rules is to not *shame* yourself, your spouse, your friends, or your children. Do you know what shaming means? I didn't, and it took me a while to roll no shaming successfully into our lives. Here is a good definition of shaming regarding children:

> Shame is designed to cause children to curtail behavior through negative thoughts and feelings about themselves. It involves a comment—direct or indirect—about what the

child is. Shaming operates by giving children
a negative image about their selves [*sic*]—rather than about the impact of their behavior.

(www.naturalchild.org)

David and I were shocked at how many times situations
arose in our household where we didn't even know we were
shaming. I always thought if I said to Teddy, "Hey, look,
Wiggy has her shoes on, why don't you?" these words would
get him going. Nope, we were comparing and shaming. Who
knew? Here are some examples of shaming and how you, too,
can remove it from your everyday communication with your
kids and other people:

- A parent says to his child, "Eat your pizza." The child
  says, "No." The parent says, "Well, look at William's
  plate. He ate all his pizza and had seconds." Hmmm,
  what's the goal there? The goal of the parent in that
  situation is to get the kid to eat the pizza. But the
  path to get there is shaming. By comparing one child
  to the other, the parent is making the non-pizza-eat-
  er feel horrible about not eating pizza. This isn't
  parenting, this isn't communicating, this is not the
  path to get children, or anyone, to do what you want.
  Also, this is not letting your children listen to their
  own bodies about feeding themselves. Maybe pizza
  doesn't sound good to them.

- You are at a soccer game and you hear a parent talking
  to another parent about how awful her five-year-old
  (who is standing right there) was that morning, as if
  the child cannot hear. The child would not put on

her shoes, the child wouldn't eat her breakfast, the child wouldn't do this or that, the child is so difficult. Imagine how that little one is feeling hearing her mother say all these horrible things about her. This is shaming, folks! Yep, maybe that kid did have a bad day ... we all do. If you need a break from your children, please take one. Or if you need to get your difficult morning off your chest, just be sure to do it out of your child's earshot. And the simplest comment of "look at what my little one is wearing today" is still shaming. Celebrate your kids, folks. Celebrate your son wearing a tutu, cleats, and a camo backpack. Your kid might be the next Versace; you just never know. So skip the shaming comments. I am sure you can find something much more intelligent to talk about.

Bribe

I hear parents bribing their kids all the time. If you are saying to your kids, "If you go to soccer, you can have dessert after dinner; if you finish your dinner, you can watch TV; if you go to school on time today, you can have a playdate; if you finish the baseball season, we will go to Toys 'R' Us; if you stop crying, I will buy you a toy; if you go to sleep, you can ..." You get the point. If you are using "if-then" statements with parenting, you are bribing your kids. Just stop. You are a better, smarter parent than this. I hear so much bribing it kills me.

Bribing closes all doors of communication with your child. It doesn't allow you to teach your child that things are not always going to be as your child wishes. In a roundabout way, it puts your child in the driving seat, and your child isn't old enough to drive. You are saying to your child, "If you decide to make the right decision, I will reward you with 'x' for your accomplishments." Folks, we want to raise kids to make the right decisions without expecting a reward.

Even giving your cell phone to your child to entertain him because he is not behaving is bribing. When you bribe your child, you are relieving him of feeling any discomfort. Yes, I understand you are trying to alleviate your discomfort, but you gotta take the long position here. Think about it— your kid doesn't want to do his piano lesson, so you nudge him with a little treat at the end. Maybe you think it's mean or rude to tell your children to stick with their commitments, or it's hard to watch your children deal with "difficult" situations. Or it's difficult for you to see your little offspring unhappy. Let me break this down for you: life is *filled* to the brim with commitments, disappointments, unhappiness, and difficult situations. Teach your little offspring now that there are things they are just going to have to do and there will rarely be a piece of candy at the end. Your child's future boss will not be bribing him to complete an end-of-year report; instead, it will be expected of him. Teach your kids now.

SIDE NOTE

Up above I put "difficult" in quotes. Wonder why? Well, being forced to go to tennis, take piano lessons, go up to bat at baseball is not really a difficult situation. It is an opportunity. And you should be raising your child as such. If your little sweetheart doesn't want to do her tennis lesson, then stop paying for it and put the money toward lessons for a kid who would appreciate it. There are children all over this world who would kill to get one tennis lesson in their lifetime.

On another note, if your kid doesn't want to go to soccer, maybe you should ask him if he likes it. If your child doesn't like soccer, then don't sign him up again. Kids are forced to do so many things all day long in their lives; don't force them to play a sport they don't like. Let them choose sports or activities they like. We need to get freedom back into kids' lives and decrease this world of over-scheduling. Yes, children need exercise—but it should be fun. I think athletics for kids are out of control, but I won't hop on that soapbox just yet. Let's keep talking about bribing. Bribing your children is setting them up for a shitty life. You are teaching your children that for every single thing they do, they should get something in return. You are not raising children who will contribute to society unless society gives back to them. I know that's not your goal. I know your plan is to not raise spoiled brats. So stop bribing and start parenting.

If you bribe your children, this section about "how to stop bribing" is *not* going to be fun to read. Sadly, there are no tricks to stopping bribing. It's kinda like alcoholism or drug addiction: you just gotta stop cold turkey when you are ready to commit. Same thing with bribing; when you are ready to get on board, you are just going to have to quit cold turkey and then get on your work boots and gloves, cuz listening to your child cry, scream, and moan and groan is gonna be tough. Here are some sure-fire ways to stop bribing:

1. For starters, you must get on board and catch yourself before you are about to drop the bribe bomb and *stop*.

Do not bribe. Your kids are going to fight you when you tell them with politeness to do their homework and there is no treat for doing it. They are most likely going to ask you for the bribe … "If I do my homework, can I have seconds on dessert?" Just say, "No, I'm sorry; you need to finish your homework." Or you can let them down gently if that's a better approach for you and tell your kids, "We will see about dessert after dinner; in the meantime, finish your homework please."

2. Ask yourself why you are about to bribe. Is your child tired? Does he need help with his task? Does he not like what he is doing? For example, does your child not want to go to swimming because he doesn't like it? I know a lot of people who don't like swimming; your kid may be one of them. Is your little guy scared of the water because he fell in when he was younger? Or does your little one know that if he pitches a fit, you will reward him with a "prize" to complete his lesson? If this is the case and you are getting on the *no-bribe* train, you are going to have a tantrum on your hands. Get out your safety gear, cuz it's gonna be a big one. You have trained your little one that a little hemming and hawing generally reaps big rewards for him. Not only are you going to have a tantrum, you are going to have a bummed-out child, because he has all of sudden lost his routine reward system. So comfort him if you are just getting on this bandwagon of *no bribing*. Give your child a hug and simply say, "I'm sorry; I understand you are scared, sad, or don't know what to do." Remind yourself you created this bribing situation; your child did not. So love him on through the hard time. Do not offer him *anything*

except hugs and "I'm sorry, I understand." And then throw on your patience hat because this will probably take about three to four swimming lessons (or whatever situation you are in) to get over.

3. Talk to your child and listen. Listen to what your child wants. Maybe she doesn't want to go to piano lessons because the teacher's breath is so bad it gives her a stomachache. Maybe your child is afraid of the soccer coach. Maybe your kiddo doesn't want to do homework because she needs a little free time before she starts. Go ahead and open up the lines of communication and listen to why your child may or may not want to do something. You will probably be surprised. And, folks, the time to ask about this is not in the heat of your children saying they don't want to go. *You will not get a decent answer.* Ask when you aren't about to go to swimming, piano, school, or wherever. Ask your child an hour before the event or in the morning or the evening after the big tantrum. In the heat of the moment, you will get a ridiculous response.

If bribing has been a big part of your childrearing, you've got a bumpy road ahead of you. But the light at the end of the tunnel shines big and bright. Your children have responsibilities and commitments even at their young ages. Teach those little guys to handle it all.

SIDE NOTE

A mom at one of the kids' schools asked David and me on separate occasions how we got our children into the car and buckled up after school every day. David was dumbfounded; he didn't understand what she meant. I talked to that woman and she said she could not get her daughter into the car and buckled into her car seat unless she had a little treat or sticker or toy to bribe her daughter with. She asked me what she should do. I said you can handle it one of two ways: 1) pick the kid up and strap her into her car seat, or 2) sit on the curb outside your car with the doors unlocked and wait it out until your child is bored enough from hanging out in the parking lot to get in the car and buckle herself in. She is still bribing her child every day.

Learning for the Little Ones

Just wait to teach your kid everything. David always says, "Do you know any twenty-year-olds who are not potty trained? Or who can't read" No, you don't. Just slow it down. Don't worry about educating and teaching your kids everything before they need to know it. Let your kids learn at their pace. Let your kids ask to learn what they want to learn. We have a lot of children and I am not killing myself to teach my kids numbers and letters. If one of our children asks to learn something, I'm on board and happy and excited to teach. But for us, home is for love, great experiences, and spending time together. Maybe you cook with your children every now and then, maybe you do gardening with your kids, maybe your five-year-old is begging to learn to read, maybe your six-year-old is finally ready to ride a bike. Teach them! They will be like sponges, learning in a second. But don't whip out the letter flashcards for your two-year-old. Don't force your little one to do soccer. Teach your kiddos the love of learning by teaching them, when they want and ask to learn. Trust me, they will ask. Your kids will not only gain a love for learning, they will find out that they are capable of learning anything they set their minds to. And I think that is one of the best lessons you can teach your kids.

Cool your jets. I'm not saying don't teach your children anything or steer away from it if the opportunity presents itself. Instead, I'm saying *relax*. Your children will learn to read, they will figure out their numbers. Don't worry if your kid heads to kindergarten and can't write his name; he will learn it. Just enjoy your little nuggets.

"You're Okay"

This is my biggest pet peeve when it comes to parenting: *telling a crying child, "You're okay."* Why would you do this? Because you think it's going to make your child feel better quicker, and that he will hopefully stop crying? Last time I checked, no one has figured out how to feel exactly the same way another person feels, not even Google. So if your kid is hurt or sad or mad, don't tell him he is "okay" or "it's okay." If your kid spills his milk and he is screaming and crying about it, don't tell him it's no big deal ... cuz obviously it is. Instead, tell your child you are sorry he spilled his milk and help him clean it up.

SIDE NOTE

Do you see how you can sneak in the "I'm sorry" when your child is upset? Now, that is the way to teach I'm sorry. Your kid is bummed and you tell him you are sorry he is bummed. Or you tell him you understand. And then you can offer to help him clean up the mess. Think about it this way ... one glass of spilled milk gives you the opportunity to apologize to your child because he spilled his milk, and you are teaching empathy. Second, you offer to help your child clean up the milk. You are modeling great behavior, teaching your child to help others and you can teach your child how to properly clean up a spill. All of that with one glass of spilled milk.

There is no simpler way to diminish someone's feelings than to dismiss them. So next time your kid skins her knee or is told "no," or is just upset because she is upset, please, please, please, I beg you ... *do not say*, "You are okay," or, "It's okay." Instead, tell her you are sorry for her or that you understand, and offer to help her out. And, remember, the only reason you are telling your kid "you are okay" is because you want them to be okay so you don't have to deal with the crying.

- If your child has fallen for the fourth time that morning. Bite your tongue or pinch yourself and give him another hug. Don't say "you are okay." Sorry, but you don't know how your kid feels—you don't. Your kid might be screaming because he is embarrassed and he hasn't conquered that vocabulary yet. So a simple "I'm sorry, I understand" from his parent could be the most comforting thing you could give your child. And you should want to support your kids' feelings, not squash them. So just grab that crying child and give him a hug and tell him you are sorry. And don't follow your "I'm sorry" with an "I told you not to run down the stairs"; that's shaming. Just "I'm sorry" and then bite your tongue so you don't wreck a beautiful moment of comforting a crying child.

- If the clothes your kid wants to wear are not clean or too small and she is upset, help her! Don't tell her "it's okay." Say you are sorry for her and be there to support her and help her find something else to wear.

So leave "it's okay" and "you are okay" out of your vocabulary when you are dealing with your children or anyone. Like I said, science and technology have not advanced enough so that you can feel someone else's feelings.

Don't Bring a Toy

Our kids don't bring toys with them when we leave the house. We don't bring stuffed animals, crayons, stickers, dolls, cars, books, their favorite security stuffed animals, or blankets; we don't bring anything. If we are leaving the house, we are leaving it with our bodies, clothes, and diapers … no toys and no snacks. When we are leaving the house, we are headed out to enjoy life, not play with toys from home. This rule holds for vacations; we do not bring toys.

We may be headed to do something fun or not; either way, it will be experienced without the distraction of a toy. Maybe we are headed to the park, maybe we are headed to get flu shots. Wherever we are off to, my children (and yours too) can handle the world without an arsenal of toys or screens in tow. It makes me very sad when we are anywhere and a child has his head down playing with a toy or, even worse, an iPad, when there is so much in this world to see. Every outing for a child is an opportunity for the child to see and experience something new. I don't ever want to take that away from my children by allowing them to bring something from home to keep them entertained. Here are some examples:

- When we head out to a restaurant, we want to sit with our family and/or friends and enjoy each other's company. We don't want to be engrossed in toys or screens while we are paying good money to be out together and enjoy each other. Yes, there is the occasional meltdown because one of the kids gets impatient or is hungry or is having trouble sitting still. But how else am I going to teach my kids restaurant manners if I don't just drag them out there and get started on it. If I can avoid it, I don't get the crayons and coloring books offered. Our children are capable of having a decent conversation or at least listening to one. I can't tell you how many times my kids have befriended wait staff or guests sitting next to us because they are out experiencing the world and not sucked into some toy we brought from home.

- When we head to the park or to watch one of our kids' sporting events, we don't bring toys. Yes, if my husband is coming with us there generally is a ball in the mix. But, other than that, no stuffed animals or crayons or snacks travel with us. We are there to play at the park and/or watch sports. Oftentimes, other families have toys, coloring books, or food they bring along with them, and my kids sometimes migrate over there; that's okay too.

- When we head to a friend's house, we do not bring our own toys. I know sometimes it's exciting to show off a new toy, but I want my kids to focus on the excitement of their visit to a friend's house. And even if we are heading to the house of someone who does not have kids, I still don't bring toys along. I want our children to find entertainment in life, in people, in new places, in new experiences. I don't want our kids to be self-centered and focused on their toys. I would never head to a friend's house for a visit completely engrossed in a new app on my phone, and I don't allow my kids to do it either.

- We don't bring toys on trips. With the car seats, strollers, and luggage for all of us, I am not adding toys to the mix. I do let the kids bring their sleeping pals, but the toys stay home. Our kids get pretty creative hanging out with each other, exploring, and just running around. And the best part is that when they get home it's like Christmas—they are so excited to see their toys and their bedrooms.

- Cell phones. To date, only one of our children has a cell phone. He is not allowed to bring it to the dinner table or to his bedroom on school nights.

I think you get the point. In short, I travel light (except for the number of kids with me); I only bring kids and diapers, no food or toys. And to give you a gauge, starting at age one, all of our children have been able to sit in a highchair at a restaurant without a toy for an hour without an issue. Your children can do the same.

Offer to Help

SIDE NOTE

If someone walked in on you and your significant other while you were fighting and told you to stop, what would you do? Wait until they left and then continue to fight, right? But if someone walked in and offered to help you with your argument, what would you do? You would lose the tension in your shoulders and relax because you had someone to help you navigate your difficult situation and each of your sides of the story could be heard by a neutral party.

We offer to help our kids out. You are probably thinking, "Wow, good for you!" It's a little different than that, and it's one of my favorite parenting tools. Here's how it works:

The kids are starting to ramp up into a fight. It's at about 10 mph, then we hit 30 mph, and at about 44 mph—before the screaming—I step in and say, "Can I help you guys?" I don't tell them not to fight, I don't start punishing. I don't scream at them to take it somewhere else. Instead, I ask, "Can I help you guys?" They are familiar with this program. They know I'm not there to punish but to start helping them work through whatever they are dealing with. But that's only if they want me to help. There are times when they are yelling at each other and I will offer to help them and they say, "No, we are okay." Other times, they need a lot of help. And I help.

When you offer to help your children communicate or help them navigate a frustrating situation, you are doing them a huge favor for the rest of their lives. You are teaching your children how to help others as you are helping them. And like I said before, you have a great opportunity to teach your kids better communication.

SIDE NOTE

A while ago, David and I were getting ready for a party. You know how it is when you are trying to get something done (whatever it may be) and you continue to get interrupted—it's very aggravating. Wiggy had gone to the basement to get some art supplies to work with in the kitchen. She couldn't carry it all upstairs by herself. Instead of asking for help, she laid face down on the floor in the basement, crying and screaming. "Irritated" does not come close to describing how I was feeling. Instead of yelling at her to get up off the floor and stop crying, I gritted my teeth, walked downstairs, and asked her if I could help. I knew what the problem was. Her art supplies were scattered around her; it was obvious. She looked up and said through the tears that she could not carry everything upstairs. I said, "Would you like me to help?" She said yes and together we carried everything upstairs. She was coloring in no time and happy as could be. Sure, I could have used this situation to punish her for crying about something that was so little. But she was clearly upset; she must have worked very hard to gather all of her supplies and was really looking forward to working on her project. So next time you find your kids in a jam, before you punish, offer to help them out and see where it takes you.

And once you start offering to help your kids, you just might hear the same words roll off their tongues. Because we are always offering to help our kids all the time, they are continuously offering to help each other.

Here is why offering to help your kids works so great:

- When war breaks out in our house, I don't immediately punish; I offer to help. Our kids don't fear me walking into a room when they are arguing. Instead, I am offering an olive branch to them, and they are eager to speak up and be heard. This does not mean I won't be punishing children for poor behavior; I can still do that, but *first*, I may need to offer some help to hear the whole story, give a hug, or help them communicate.

- Because we are constantly offering to help our kids, they are always offering to help each other.

- When the kids get in arguments with each other, they have been taught to ask for help rather than engage in the argument. So rather than Harvey taking a swing at Wiggy, he is working on asking for help from David or myself to work through things with Wiggy.

- When we offer to help the kids, rather than immediately punish them, I instantly calm down, and so do they. So the next time your little ones or teenagers (or even your husband) is losing it, just offer to help and see what happens.

- When our kids spill milk, or their dinner slides off their plates as they are carrying it to the table, and the tears erupt, we offer to help them clean it up. We do not say, "It's okay" because from the tears and screams, I can tell it clearly isn't. Instead, we help diffuse the situation by offering to help them clean up the mess. And we give them a lesson in cleaning at the same time.

Oh, and for the record, if you are wondering whether or not I handle these little situations at my house perfectly every time, you can rest your head at night knowing the answer is *absolutely not* ... but I wish I did.

Whispering to Your Kids

When I was a commodities trader, I spent a lot of time in human resources because of my vocabulary. There wasn't a mass email sent out to the trading floor explaining that Kysa Alport (maiden name) had a swearing problem. No, an email was sent to me only, asking me to visit human resources. I took the stairs up one floor, went into a private room with my boss, and we both fought human resources about my vocabulary.

At school, when you get in trouble, most of the time it is discussed in private. So it's time to discipline your children privately. Nobody needs to hear that your child is in trouble. So the next time you are in public and your little guy decides to misbehave (or, like I saw a child do yesterday, throw his backpack in his mom's face), just quietly tell your little one what he did was wrong. No need to say it so *everyone* can hear that your little offspring made a poor choice. No one cares, and it's also another form of shaming. No lessons are learned when you shame and embarrass your kids. And the world doesn't want to know that your child is misbehaving.

Let Your Kids Be

This is so simple, and yet so easy to screw up. If your children are happily playing or relaxing or doing whatever they are doing, and they are content, happy, quiet, not asking for anything ... *do not bother them; just let them be*. Here are some examples:

- If your kids are coloring and they only have one pen, don't offer them more. Let them be creative doing different patterns with one color, sharing the pen, or maybe coloring a tree pink. Just let them enjoy what they are doing; just let them be.

- If your kids are outside playing soccer with a basketball, don't tell them they should get a soccer ball. Just let them be. Don't interrupt them, don't change their game, don't change their program. They came up with a game, let them enjoy it.

- If your children are sitting on the couch relaxing, let them be. Don't offer them a drink, don't offer them a snack. In this day and age, it is important to not only teach our kids to relax, but to let them do it!

- If your little ones are building a tower, and it has fallen over for the eighth time, and your children are still smiling, don't offer to help, because you will end up building it for them. Your kids are so happy with the process, let them enjoy it. (Of course, if you are asked for help, then help. Otherwise let them be.)

You get the point. Let your kids be in charge of their play, their down-time, their whatever-time. There is *no need* to offer more when they *do not* ask you for anything.

By doing this, you will be teaching your little ones to ask for what they need, rather than offering them what they need before they know they need it. I'll say it again: let your children be. Let them ask for what they need.

SIDE NOTE

I set up a game for our kids to play indoor basketball with socks. I tied a string between two dining room chairs (they were supposed to stand behind the string). I then set up a bunch of mixing bowls on the other side of the string. They were supposed to throw socks in the bowls. Instead, they decided to throw socks at the string between the two chairs. It was a much harder game than I came up with, and they were happy as clams. I let them be.

No Sharing Allowed

Have you ever watched your child have to share her toy with another kid? She gives the death stare until she gets it back.

Until age five-ish, I don't teach or force our kids to share their toys. Instead, I take the opportunity to work on communication. Here's an example: Teddy is working away with magnetic tiles constructing a masterpiece, and Wiggy comes over wanting to build something too. Instead of forcing Teddy to "share" the tiles with her, I ask Wiggy to ask Teddy if she can also play with the tiles. Sometimes he says yes, and sometimes he says no. This way I can stay out of it and they have another opportunity to work on communication. If Teddy says "no" and Wiggy is really upset, she can either ask him for a few tiles, or ask to play with them when he is done. If the answer is still "no," then I help Wiggy find a project of her own to work on, or have her hang out with me.

When a child is working so nicely (like Teddy was in the example), I want him to keep at his project. And I want Wiggy to respect his space. I get it: Teddy's magnetic tile building is very enticing, and I can see why Wiggy wants to join him. It's an opportunity where Wiggy can learn to ask permission, respect others' space, and learn patience while she waits to play with the tiles. Teddy gets to think about what he really wants and speak up about it—"No, you cannot join me right now," he can tell her. The whole scenario works itself out nicely.

Let's look at it as if the tables were turned. If I forced Teddy to share the tiles with Wiggy, his space would be invaded. He would need to share tiles he already had a plan for, and I would upset his program. Wiggy would most likely be a little pissed off too, because Teddy would still have some of the tiles she wanted. And no great lessons would be learned.

Of course, I do think sharing is important. I have chosen to use food to teach our children the concept. Often they will sit down for lunch or breakfast or dinner and I will load up one plate of food. I call it a "snack plate." A "snack plate" is not "snacks"; it's when I'm too busy or unprepared to make a real meal: I just throw a bunch of healthy food on a plate and call it a snack plate. My kids love it. When our children get a snack plate they take a few things and pass the plate. They have to share the plate of food. And if they are hungry, this can really be tough for them. But I quickly remind them that if we need to refill the plate, we can. They do a great job asking for the plate and passing it back and forth to each other. And the best part about it is that I don't have to force them to share; they are just naturally doing it. It's an easier way to teach sharing at their ages.

Sports & Activities & Attitude

Teddy, Wiggy, and Harvey take tennis lessons. The lessons are very mellow and close to our house, and the kids have a lot of fun. For a while, when I picked Teddy up from school, he asked what we were doing. On the days with tennis, he pitched a fit—but when he got to tennis, he raced to the court and had a blast. I ignored his behavior for a while. Then I changed my tune. We pay for his tennis lessons. One evening when he didn't have tennis I asked him what was going on and why he always got upset before tennis. He didn't have an answer, so I asked him if he wanted to continue with tennis. He said yes. I told him I expected him to be polite to me after school or he wasn't going to participate in tennis. The next time I picked him up, he hemmed and hawed about tennis. I said, "No tennis today." He was stoked. He said, "I'm going to watch TV in the lobby." I told him he would be sitting on the bench watching his tennis lesson. He sat there quietly and watched his tennis lesson for 45 minutes. He didn't ask to join; he just sat there quietly and watched. I wanted him to understand that tennis is a privilege and that he is not going to be rewarded for a bad attitude and certainly not for being rude to me. I want our children to respect the lives we provide for them. I'm not going to drive kids all over town for activities they bitch and moan about doing. I am not going to waste money and time to push a child to do a sport/activity he is bitching and moaning about.

The following Tuesday I picked Teddy up from school and he asked what we were doing and I said tennis. He smiled and kept on walking to the car. His attitude has been that way ever since.

So what's my takeaway here? If your kids don't want to do a sport, then you probably shouldn't be forcing them to do it. Why waste money and time driving them around to something they don't want to do? Our children choose their activities. And, yes, sometimes they choose activities they don't end up liking. That's okay too; that has happened to me. I have had a five-pack of yoga in my wallet for almost a year. It happens. But I will use up my yoga classes and your child should finish up what they start. The great thing is that your children are trying out new things and figuring out what they do and don't like. You want to support that. You want to support your children speaking up about what they do and don't like; they just need to do it politely.

We Do Not Give Our Children Warnings

You will never hear me say, "If you do that again, you are going to have a seat on the stair." My kids are going to the stair the first time, every time. I don't think kids need warnings; I think they know what's wrong and right. Here are some examples:

- David was out BBQing and Teddy had his toys dumped out near the BBQ. David was keeping a close eye on him, but he knew what was going to happen. Daddy was playing with the BBQ and Teddy wanted to play to. I watched it happen; Teddy put his hand out to touch the BBQ. We could have stood there warning Teddy and reminding him how hot the BBQ was. We would have been chasing him around and reminding him all evening. Instead, we let him learn on his own. I would never do this with anything life-threatening, of course—a street, a campfire, or a pool, for instance. But the BBQ worked. Today Teddy will tell you BBQs are very hot.

- When Ian is heading out with friends, we don't tell Ian not to be late. We tell him when to come home. If he is one minute late, he knows he won't be able to join in the next activity with his friends. Ian has a phone, and he knows how to use it, and if he is going to be late, he needs to let us know. There is absolutely no reason for us to worry. And, frankly, there is absolutely no reason for a teenager to be late.

- Our children know the rules at our dinner table. No throwing food, no banging dishware, no loud voices, etc. If any one of those rules are broken, the offending child is asked to leave the table. That child's dinner is over. A warning isn't necessary; it just falls on deaf ears.

Don't give your children warnings. You may need to remind your child of the rules from time to time, and that's okay. But don't hand out warnings. Life doesn't give you warnings.

How to Get Your Kids to Clean Up

I'm *not* a professional, but I do have a few tricks up my sleeve to get our kids to clean up after themselves.

- First and foremost, you (moms, dads, caregivers) need to keep a clean home. You cannot be nagging your children to clean up after themselves if the rest of the house isn't tidy.
- You need to have a place for your children (any age) to put things away. If the items in your home don't have a home, how can anyone clean up? Everything needs to have its own drawer, basket, bin, or cupboard. Art supplies, craft paper, dolls, doll clothes, stuffed animals, Legos, blankets, and sports equipment all need to have a home. If you are having trouble finding these spots in your home, call your most organized friend and have her come over and get you on track.
- You need to de-clutter.
- Lead by example. If you clean, your kids will clean.

Cleaning a house and keeping it clean requires tons and tons and tons of constant work and attention. It takes everyone pitching in to keep a home clean and tidy. Our house is almost always spotless, and that's because everyone pitches in.

When I moved in with David, Ian was seven years old. Right away, I wanted Ian to start pulling his weight around the house. Yes, I was the girlfriend who moved in and insisted on chores for Ian. I kept it very simple in the beginning. I started with having him make his bed. He did it when I reminded him, but when I stopped reminding him, he stopped. If his bed wasn't made when we got home from school, I would have him do it. I just smiled and said, "It needs to be done." He would rant and rave that he was going to bed soon anyway. I stuck to my guns, and finally, he figured out a routine and remembered to make his bed in the morning. Some time ago, I saw Ian making his bed after school. I leaned into his room and said, "Thank you." Consistency, folks, consistency.

Here's how I keep a spotless home:

- I have made it *very* easy for the kids to clean up. There is a place for *everything*. We do not have piles of toys in the corners of our rooms. If this is happening at your house, *it is time for Goodwill*. We have bins or shelves for their toys. Like I said, there is a place for *everything*. If it's hard for you to clean your kids' toys up because there isn't enough room for everything, imagine how your kids feel. It's overwhelming. So it's time to gather the team and go through the old toys. No need to force the kids to get rid of everything, but it is time to clean out. You can easily get rid of broken toys and those with lost parts, and you can pass unwanted toys along.

- Laundry. Our children either have a laundry basket in their rooms or one nearby. They are to put their dirty clothes in the laundry if they would like them cleaned. Our kids know they can't wear the same clothes two days in a row, so there is no point in leaving dirty clothes in their rooms.

- Our children's beds are very easy to make. They have a fitted sheet and comforter—no flat sheet, no blanket, just a nice, cozy comforter. All they have to do is pull up the comforter and straighten it out. Very simple. I do this every morning, and I expect them to do the same. Our children move into big beds at age four, so at age four they are required to make their beds. In the beginning, I get on one side of the bed and they get on the other, and together we pull the comforter up and straighten it out. I will do this for about a week. After that, I have them do the best they can and then I can go in and offer a hand to get it just right. A few weeks into this program, they are on their own, with gentle reminders from time to time.

- Sometimes our kids need a little encouragement to start cleaning. If we are in the basement, we play "toy basketball," throwing the toys into the bins. Sometimes I even line up all the bins so they can score points easier. And sometimes I have to shoot and score and hoot and holler a few times to get them started. And, yes, sometimes I have to clean up with them. My goal is not to yell at them to clean up, but to kindly encourage them to clean up. Yes, I do get frustrated with them from time to time. But I always try to keep my workforce happy; I encourage them to clean rather than nag or yell at them to do it.

- Another thing I do is tell them we can't leave for the park or have dinner or go outside until everything is cleaned up. I say it kindly—always keep your workforce happy. This approach usually gets a lot of hems and haws, but they know I stick to my word and we cannot leave until the mess is cleaned up. The same goes for Ian. He doesn't get to leave for his events until his chores or duties are completed, and completed properly.

- If the kids have really wrecked the house, I give everyone a zone. Here's an example of how it works. Teddy takes the kitchen zone; he cleans up all the toys in the kitchen. Wiggy is on patrol in the living room, cleaning up from a book party they had. And Harvey takes the basement. It works well.

- Your kids can clean up. It's like their clothing; if they got the toys out, they can put the toys back. Sure, sometimes they may need help, but they can be present and helping until the job is done.

So just keep encouraging your little workforce. Assist them, love them, and slowly remove yourself from the cleaning process. And don't forget, you don't always want to clean up the house, and neither will they. It's okay. You keep a clean house and your children will keep a clean house too. Just work together and remember the end goals are to have children who pick up after themselves and to *decrease your workload*. Be kind, loving, and supportive—no nagging. And, remember, when you have to help your workforce, that's okay. You are modeling good habits by "helping others," and spending quality time with your young'uns.

SIDE NOTE

I don't go to bed at night until every square inch of the house is picked up. If everyone has done their share and cleaned up after themselves throughout the day, this should not be a big job. It rarely takes more than fifteen minutes for me to zip around the house and tidy everything up. I always go to bed with the dishwasher running and the washing machine going.

Don't Cut the Crusts Off Your Kids' Sandwiches ... and All the Other "Firsts" We Need to Avoid

Do you ever wonder how it started that a child, or anyone for that matter, doesn't like crust on a sandwich? I don't get it; most of the time crust tastes the same as the other part of the bread. I can understand people not liking pizza crust, because it is missing all the yummy toppings. But sandwich crust? Come on. Someone needed to say "no" a long time ago and not cut kids' crusts off their sandwiches. Just say, "I'm sorry, the crust comes with the bread." That's the end of the story; no need to do any extra work, just leave the crust on. This leads me to a lot of other "firsts" we as parents should just say "no" to:

- Not wearing underwear. We've already gone over this, but let's have another crack at it anyway. I have heard of kids who don't like wearing underwear. I know some adults don't like to wear underwear either; that's fine (kinda). But kids should wear underwear, and someone should have just said, "I'm sorry, we wear underwear between our bodies and our clothes." And when your child complains about wearing underwear, tell them you are sorry but you know their bodies will soon get used to it. If you nip this one in the beginning, it will not be an issue. If you don't, you may find your son doesn't like to have his shoes laced up because it's uncomfortable. Not safe. You may find your 15-year-old with a C-cup doesn't want to wear a bra because it's uncomfortable. The bottom line is that sometimes things are uncomfortable—but eventually, our bodies get used to them.

- Your kid has to have a particular utensil or cup to eat with at every meal. Do not start this madness. Just say, "Oops, I'm sorry, that isn't available right now." Yes, you will get the screams and rants, but ignore them; it's okay for your child to be upset. Your child may go on a starvation diet until they get what they want; they won't last on that diet. Kids don't like hunger—no one does. Do not lose this battle. And please don't think buying Hello Kitty or Superman dishware is going to make your children better eaters. It will not. They will have more fun playing with their food, pushing it to the side so they can see the famed characters. And may I also point out that the special dishware to get your bad eater to eat is another form of bribery. You are saying, "Here, sweetie, you are a bad eater so I'm going to give you this awesome dish set that I will slave over to make sure it always clean to meet your needs at every meal." Hell no.

I think you get the point. If what your child is asking for with regularity is a little ridiculous and giving you extra work, you should be saying *no*. There is a great litmus test here: quickly ask yourself, is it *normal* for my child to be going to bed with every light on in her room, for her not to wear underwear, for him not to eat his food if it is touching, etc.? If the demands are a bit too much, or if you heard another parent saying this about his child, would you be rolling your eyes? If so, then a simple, polite, and loving "no" is okay. You don't need to say, "It's okay your food is touching." Instead, say, "I'm sorry your food is touching." Period.

It all boils down to discomfort. Discomfort is okay. Parenting is not paving a diamond path with golden handrails for our children. Parenting is about joy, pain, sorrow, learning, experiencing, loving, and so on. Don't feel misery so your child does not have to. Your children will have a very difficult life if they don't get the opportunity to start feeling and experiencing difficulties and discomfort now. Life is tough, and if you can dose out a few (or many) hardships at home with love and support, your child will be a better person for it. And ... drumroll please ... in the long run, this will make parenting easier. So don't cut the crust off your kid's PB & J.

Screaming Kids in the Car

Have you ever experienced this? I have. It makes it very difficult to drive. And, yes, I do want to turn around and scream back at my kids, and I have. But you shouldn't; remember, we are supposed to *model* decent behavior for our children. If my kids take their voices up to a volume that I just can't deal with, I simply pull the car over and don't say a word— remember, less talking. And, yes, I have had to pull over more than once while driving to and from school sometimes. Often, it takes a bit for my kids to realize we are stopped, but I just grab my phone and check emails until someone asks why we aren't moving. I give the same answer every time: "I can't drive when you scream." This works very, very well, especially if someone is going to be late to a friend's house, birthday party, school, or whatever. The screaming stops quickly.

As a chauffeur to our children, I expect respect in my car. Not only do our children get a free ride in the car, I pay for the gas too! So they can shape up or ship out.

SIDE NOTE

Not too long ago, I had had it with Teddy, and I kicked him out at the corner to walk home. He was five and it was raining and he didn't have a jacket. Thankfully, David was in the car and joined him for his stroll home. I would not have done it without David, but I would have been close that day. Our children are very fortunate to have the cars we do and the rides we are willing to give them. They are going to learn to appreciate and respect us for it. If they can't, they won't be riding in our cars.

I had the same situation with Ian years ago. He was always ticked off about having to go to soccer practice. Let me tell you, at that time, it was not a picnic for me. I had to load Teddy (age one and not walking) and Wiggy (a baby) in the car while pregnant with Harvey, and pick up four other boys for soccer carpool during dinnertime. One particular evening, I told Ian to get ready for soccer, and he bitched and moaned, and I said, "Fine, I'm not taking you." I called the other parents to apologize because I couldn't do carpool that evening. Ian missed soccer. He was shocked and, surprisingly, pissed. But I was tired of his attitude, and to me it didn't seem like he enjoyed soccer. Ian still does soccer, and guess what I hear every time I take him to practice, "Thanks for the ride, Kys." That's the way it should be.

Forget ... "Can You"

When you ask *anyone* (especially kids) to do something, leave out the "can you" portion in the beginning of your question and replace it with "please." Instead of saying, "Can you go put your shoes on?" say, "Please go put your shoes on." This may seem like a nuance, but it's not. When you say to your kids, "Can you go put your shoes on?" you are phrasing it as a question. But you shouldn't be asking a question, because you would like them to put their shoes on. When you say, "Please go put your shoes on," you do not pose it as a question; it is a command. Your children can still say "no," but you simply say it again and again and again, and finally, they will get tired of hearing it and go put their shoes on. This little trick can be used anywhere in your life, but it is really handy with kids and other family members. It's kind of weird at first, and also hard to remember, but once you start getting the hang of it, you will see a nice, efficient change in your home and other areas of your life.

So leave out the "can you" and start saying "please." By using the word "please," this is also another way of modeling good manners.

Patience

Parenting and patience are two words that don't always go hand in hand. It is very hard to have patience when you have witnessed spilled milk twice in twenty minutes, stepped in dog pee, heard someone fall down the stairs, changed a blowout, and are trying to cook dinner. I don't have patience, not an ounce. I'm Italian, and most of the time I'm a little bit pissed off about something. So for me, this part of parenting is a challenge. But I have a few tricks up my sleeve to get through the tough times.

When I was pregnant with number five, the baby we lost at four months, I didn't have any patience. I had a 14-year-old, a 5-year-old, a 3-year-old, a 2-year-old, and two dogs. To say I was going crazy was an understatement. But I had to get a handle on it or none of us were going to make it through my pregnancy. I had to get a plan in place, quick. One morning, I was trying to stay calm as Harvey was struggling and crying while trying to put his sock on. One problem was his belly; it was so big he couldn't reach his foot. The other problem was that the Elmo on his sock was on the inside, so he couldn't see it when he finally got his sock on. There was a lot of stress and frustration and screaming. But at age two, those were his stressors; those were some of the things that got him off his rails. That morning, I got on Harvey's side—I got some mommy empathy and helped him figure out a way to get his sock on, and taught him how to turn it right-side out.

Instead of getting frustrated with Harvey, I put myself in his shoes. I quickly realized how frustrating it would be to not be able to put on your own sock. And, actually, I had been there three times with my pregnancies. At some point in all pregnancies, your belly gets too big to put on your own socks, and it's frustrating. I also know how frustrating it is when you can't find the right clothes to wear, or when you think what you put on doesn't look right. I have felt all the same feelings Harvey felt about getting dressed, and I am 42. But at my age, I know how to solve my problems: when I am pregnant, I wear shoes I can slip into without socks. If what I am wearing doesn't look right, like Harvey's Elmo, I know to wear something different, or how to fix my clothes. At age two, those answers don't come so easily, or at all. So that morning I rallied my patience; I sat down on the floor with Harvey and I just helped him out. I didn't get mad at him for slowing down our morning. I taught him to solve his problems. I empowered him, and we both won.

Next time your little one is struggling, put yourself in his shoes; slow down and your patience will come—or else dig deep for it. It will help even more if you can sit down next to your kiddo to help him out. It's a nice way for you to get to his level.

Taking the Kids to Eat in Public

Taking the kids out to eat in public or to a friends' is a big adventure and sometimes a scary one. If you have one kiddo under the age of six months and she is still in the bucket car seat, you should be going out to eat a lot. Because once that little bugger grows out of that bucket and into a real car seat and is forced to sit in a highchair at restaurants, the experience changes. I'm not saying it changes for the worse, always—but it changes. Don't be afraid of restaurants or visiting friends; just learn how to do it.

You may be wondering why I recommend taking children out to eat. The answer is that we like going out to eat and we love spending time with our children—so why not kill two birds with one stone? Our children are required to sit at the table during mealtime, whether we're in our home or at a restaurant. It's actually easier for them to stay put at a restaurant, because there is so much more to see, hear, and smell. Restaurants are highly entertaining, and our children love going out. Years ago, we used to head out to dinner with two cars. If one of our little buggers wasn't cooperating, one of us would take that child home, bath her, and put her to bed. We apply the same rules at home as we do at restaurants: if you can't behave, you don't get to stay at the table.

Here are our rules and how we got to where we are now. We can take all of our children to a restaurant. They can all order for themselves, sit in their own chairs politely, and enjoy a nice dinner with us.

1. In the beginning, when the kids were younger, I used to call ahead and order the kids food as take-out. When we got to the restaurant, I would grab the kids' takeout food and sit down at our table. The kids were happy eating their food. Since kids take a bit longer to eat, the timing worked out perfectly. They were finished eating by the time our food arrived and they would place their dessert order. Super easy. Sometimes it was hard for me to explain to the person on the phone at the restaurant that I was going to order takeout but also sit down at the restaurant. Sometimes, I just left the latter part out. If we were going to an establishment that required reservations, I often made two phone calls. The first phone call was for our reservation and the second phone call was to place our takeout order—again, it was just easier to not confuse the person on the phone.

2. Unless we are going to dinner with another family, we rarely go to places where there is a play area. We want our children to learn to sit at a table, keep their voices down, and enjoy their meal.

3. If I can avoid it, I don't allow the kids to get the crayons and coloring books that are offered. Again, I want them to enjoy the atmosphere and chat with us. I don't make a big deal about this, but if I see the hostess grabbing crayons, I'll try to get her attention and let her know we don't need them.

4. You know this already; we do not take toys or iPads out with us. Nor do we let our children use our phones. We are all heading out to dinner to enjoy time with each other and give me a night off from cooking. Our children wouldn't be able to enjoy

each other or us if they were engaged with a toy they
brought from home.

5. All of our children order their own food. I make sure
they each know what they want before the server
comes to our table. If I have a kid hemming and
hawing and wasting the server's time, we quickly
move onto the next kid and allow them to order.
I will let the child who didn't order have another
opportunity to order—and if he doesn't order, he
doesn't get food. I don't want my children wasting
other people's valuable time; it's rude. Sometimes
we steer clear of the kids' menu; the choices are rarely healthy. In that case, we order a couple of adult
entrees for the children to share.

You can do this. Take your little ones out to dinner. No,
they will not always behave, but eventually, they will get the
hang of it. We get compliments every time we take the crew
out to dinner. It wasn't always easy, but now it's a breeze, and
our children love going out. And they also know that if they
don't behave, they will be heading home.

Reading Time

Almost every night David or I read to our kids. We all sit on
our bed. The children enjoy it and we love it. However, it
can be frustrating when they are wiggling around, bugging
each other, and occasionally falling off the bed. To avoid this,
I place three pillows far away from each other on our bed. I
assign each kid a pillow to sit on. If the children move off
their pillows, they are sent to bed.

Sleep

Besides love and support, I think the next best thing you can give your child is sleep, and lots of it. From the day that little one comes into the world, you should begin supporting a healthy sleep program for your child. There are numerous books on this subject, and there are numerous programs to implement in your family. I recommend doing a little research to figure out a program that you know you will be able to implement in your home. However, if you are having trouble getting your child to bed at night, I recommend hiring someone or finding a friend to come to your home to help you find a system that works for you. Just for reference: you should be able to put children who are as young as nine months old in bed and walk out the door in about one minute. Of course, you should be reading to your child, snuggling, and so on—but there are also those rushed evenings. So make sure your children understand that when it's time for bed, it's time for bed.

Our children all stay in their cribs until age four. On their fourth birthdays, they get big beds—not toddler beds, big beds. I think toddler beds are a waste of money; it's a crib without fencing. I am always surprised by the families who move their child to a toddler bed because they have a newborn on the way and don't want to purchase another crib, but instead, they purchase a toddler bed that will last for a year, at which time a larger bed needs to be purchased. Buy a second crib, folks. Keep them caged as long as you can. They are not in any pain in a crib and they fit the crib (a toddler bed uses a crib mattress). Keep your children in cribs until their head is touching one end and their toes the other.

If your children are crawling out of their cribs, I have one thing to say … I'm sorry. I saw Teddy try to crawl out of his crib once, and I told him we don't do that. He listened. Another time I was cooking dinner in the kitchen and I heard a loud thud above me from Wiggy's room; then I heard a lot of screaming (not the screaming that meant she was hurt—there's a difference). I waited about 20 minutes and went up there. I didn't say a word—the lesson had already been learned. She wasn't hurt, but she had scared the crap out of herself when she climbed out and fell. I once saw Harvey attempt to climb out of his crib and I told him to stop. If your little one attempts to get out of her crib, don't say a word. Just pick her up and put her back. Repeat as often as needed. Never, ever say a word. Just keep plopping her back in her bed. Your child will eventually get the point.

Teach your children to love sleep. I love sleep, David loves sleep, Ian loves sleep, and so do Wiggy, Harvey, and Teddy. We have taught our children that bedtime is not a punishment. When our kids don't want to go down for their naps or bedtime, I tell them sleep is one of the best things they can give their bodies. And since we are always teaching our children to take care of themselves, they are learning that sleep is one of the ways to do that.

SIDE NOTE

David taught me to sleep-train our children. When I was nursing Teddy, I remember the nurse said to feed him every three hours. So when I got home from the hospital, I put on a digital watch. I set the timer for three hours. I always knew how much time I had before the next feeding, and I always woke Teddy to feed him. I figured he needed to eat. I wanted to keep him on his feeding schedule, and keeping him on a feeding schedule would teach him to fall back asleep. Sometimes I had to pinch him (gently) or use a cold washcloth to wake him up to feed him, but he woke up every time.

When it was time to sleep-train him, David taught me to let him cry it out. I know, I know—lots and lots of reputable PhDs say not to let them cry it out. But I did it and it worked very well for our family. It was difficult to hear our little ones cry—so like any good mama, I grabbed a cocktail and headed out to the porch while they worked out their kinks and fell asleep. I learned that if Teddy cried for longer than 22 minutes, there was something wrong, so I would go up and check on him. If Wiggy cried longer than 45 minutes, I went to check on her; sometimes she needed a diaper change. And Harvey? I don't remember how long it took him. We had to sleep-train him twice. Here is the part that is going to send you over the edge (yeah, it gets worse): our children were sleep-trained either in our attic or basement. Don't worry, both are nicely finished spaces, and we could hear them on the monitors, but they were not right next to us stressing us out or waking up the other kids.

Here are some sleeping tips to get you started:

- Learn your babies' sleeping cues. I don't remember the little ones' sleep clues when they were babies, but I do remember Ian's. When Ian was younger, he would stare off into space when he was tired. That was our cue he was in need of an early bedtime. Today, Teddy does the same thing when he's tired; he stares into no-man's land. Harvey gets very teary and Wiggy will just ask to go to bed when she is tired.

• Don't let your children highjack bedtime by telling you they are thirsty or hungry right as you tuck them into bed. It's just a ploy; they don't need anything but to shut their beautiful little eyes and go to sleep. Be polite and tell your little ones it's time for bed and they can have something to drink and eat in the morning, at breakfast. Don't shame your little ones by telling them they should have drunk more or eaten more at dinner. Those are useless words only meant to hurt. You aren't teaching any lessons.

• Before you start reading time, make a clear plan of how many books you are reading, what books you are reading, and how many times you are going to read each book. Stick to your plan. When the reading is over, tell your little ones it's time for bed and you are excited to read more tomorrow night. *Do not fall for your kids begging for another book. Don't do it!*

• Tuck your little one in, give a hug, give a kiss, and walk away. *Don't crawl in bed with your kid.* Come on, folks, this is ridiculous. If you want to snuggle with your little one, carve some special time out of your busy day and do it then. Don't do it when your little one should be sleeping and you should be getting some much-needed time to yourself or with your spouse. Stay out of your children's beds.

• If your little one likes to take his pajamas and diaper off during the night, cut the feet off your child's pajamas and put them on backwards. The zipper in the back is difficult for your little one to reach.

- I can't believe I even need to write this: don't let your kids into your bed. Your bed should not be a family bed; it should be a place for you and your spouse to enjoy each other, not your children. Children do not improve any couples' sex life; don't decrease the frequency even more by adding children between your sheets. Enjoy your children during the day, folks, not at night.

Yes, I know these tips are brutal. We put our children to bed at 7:00 p.m. every night. And every evening is ours to do with as we wish. And our children wake up every morning chipper and happy to start the day. Take a long-term approach to your children and sleep. And if you can't do it yourself, that is okay. It is a very emotionally draining process. Hire someone, or wrangle in a friend to come help you.

Screen Time

Our younger children do not get it. A lot of my children's teachers have told us our children are different than most of the kids in the class. Our kids can work on a project, pay attention to story time, follow directions, and participate. I think one of the reasons is because our children are not allowed to watch TV, play on the computer, or play on our phones. Our children spend their free time doing art projects, playing outside, building forts, cooking, and just being kids. Our kids don't sit in front of the TV getting entertained, they entertain themselves.

Sure, it would probably be easier to put dinner on the table, talk on the phone, check my emails etc., if I plopped our kids in front of the TV. But I don't.

There are three situations in our children's lives where they get screen time. When they are sick, when a car ride is longer than one hour, and when we're on plane rides. In those cases, all screen time rules are out the window.

Kids ... The Morning

Getting one child out the door in the morning sometimes seems impossible. Getting four out the door is another program. Long ago I realized that school bags, lunches, socks, hats, jackets, etc., were wrecking our program. So our children have the following ready to go before they sit down for breakfast:

- Socks on.
- Shoes on.
- Jackets out and by the door.
- Lunch made and packed in their school bags.
- School bags packed and by the door.

At first it may seem like it's a lot to ask your child to be self-organized before they eat. But just try it a few times and see how easy it is to leave for school when your children are ready to go before you need to leave.

If I have a little one sit down at the table and he doesn't have his shoes on, or I see his bed isn't made, I send him away to get his work done. Of course, the kids bitch and moan—but they always do that as they are walking away to get stuff done, so I don't pay it much attention.

Your Children's Guests

Playdates can be stressful for everyone, especially your child. But first let's talk about why playdates can be stressful for parents. I'll tell you a couple of my stories. I had a little girl over to spend time with Wiggy. The girl got to our house and seemed okay. Then I heard crying; I checked on the girls and helped them solve their problem. Then I heard more crying. With every change of events, this little girl kept crying and crying. I gave her hugs, asked her if I should call her mom; I did everything I could think of. Wiggy was confused and upset. I learned three things from that playdate: one, when you have a little visitor, give her a quick tour around your house. Even if you are showing her your kitchen, point out the fridge and sink, etc. Get her comfortable and, most importantly, show her where the bathroom is. If you keep wipes in your bathroom, show your little guest where they are. Two, if the playdate goes south, do not continue to rescue it. Call the mother or caregiver and let her know the playdate is over and it's time for her child to go home. No need to blame anyone, but if you must, blame it on a migraine. And, three, if you don't know a child or his parents very well, you might want to meet at a park for the first playdate, to see if you mesh with the child and his family. After chatting with the little boy's mommy at the park, you may find out that their pit bull and gun collection don't really mesh with your family values. Or you just might make a new friend. Get to know the parents first; it's so much easier.

What does a playdate mean for your child? So much stress—you have no idea. The minute the word "playdate" is on the table for one of our kids, they instantly go into planning mode. I can practically see smoke coming out of their ears as they are plan the playdate events. When I see this happening, I quickly and gently remind my child there is going to be another person involved in the playdate and he needs to ask his friend what he wants to do when he arrives. It's like popping my kid's balloon, but it needs to happen. My children need to know that playdates include others. Teddy may want to build Legos with his buddy, but his buddy may want to play soccer. Or Wiggy might be interested in playing "family," but her friend just wants to color. Whatever it is, be aware your children and their guests may need a bit of assistance. If your child decides to be rude to you while his guest is visiting, guess whose guest is going home? I do not care about the age of your child; if your child is rude, short, or disrespectful to you when he has a guest, send the guest home. And, lastly, when it's time for that guest to leave, know that there will almost always be a water show. So help your guests leave. Walk them to the door, walk them outside, and, if needed, walk them to their cars. Just keep chatting with the crying child's caregiver as you are helping them head home.

The End

This is the end of my section on parenting. I want to end this section on this note: I read a lot. I love reading, especially biographies. There are so many amazing people on this planet, and I think most parents want to raise their children to be some of those amazing people. "Amazing" depends on what the term means to you. It could mean for your child to become the president of our country, to be in the military, to make lots of money, to be an artist, or teacher, or gymnast …

anything. For me, amazing means our children will be able to walk on this planet making their own decisions confidently and with their heads held high. Amazing means our children will be able to go for all of their dreams. I want our children to know how to think, and I want them to be polite and admit their wrongs. As for what our kids will be, I have no idea. One thing I do know is that all the "amazing" people I have read about—John Adams, Helen Keller, Grace Kelly, Henry Ford, Gandhi—the list goes on and on—all these great people have had great hardships; they have struggled and worked hard to come out successful. So please, moms, dads, and caregivers, don't pave the way for your child. Don't make your child's life so easy that it makes your life difficult. Your children can and will succeed in life, but not if you pave the perfect road for them.

Here's an example: I was at a parent meeting the other evening. I wasn't impressed, but that's not the point. All these parents were looking for answers to the most mundane parenting problems … my kids won't sit at the table, my kid colors on the furniture, my kid got mad because I carried his lunchbox. I was beside myself with these people, and so bored. These were such easy fixes. Your kids don't sit at the table? Then they must not want to eat; buckle them in or send them away with no food. Your kids color on the furniture? Take away all their pens. Your kid was mad because you carried his lunchbox? Who cares? The kicker was this: two parents were so proud of themselves when they warned their child for two days that they would have to pick him up quickly after school, rather than the usual loitering around and playing for an hour. And why did they have to do this? Why did the parents have to go to so much work to prepare their kid for a change in the normal routine? Because they thought it would make their child's life easier. Parents who break their backs to make their children's lives easier raise children whose lives become very, very hard. Why? Because these children have never, ever been given the opportunity to experience or overcome *anything* "difficult." Life is difficult. We get thrown curve balls every day. Let's raise kids who can catch the curve ball or, better yet, hit that curve ball out of the park.

Thank you for reading my book. I enjoyed writing it. It took a long time. I had to put writing and editing on hold many times. The first time I stopped writing was when I was pregnant with the twins, and got too big and uncomfortable to sit in a chair. Then I wasn't able to pick the book back up until the girls—Evelyn Judi (EJ) and Grady—were six months old. I got sidetracked again when I got too overwhelmed with the girls' feeding and sleep schedule—around seven months. Around nine months, the editor reached out to me and said the planned publishing date was around the corner. So I got back to the book.

I don't know if I will sell one copy of this book or a million. I'm just excited I stuck with it and finished it. So again, thank you for reading. Lots of love to you, your spouse, your caregivers, your children.

The next section is a bunch of tricks and tips we use around our house. All of these things have made our lives easier, and I want to share.

Warm Regards,

Kysa

The Household

Cutting Nails

Every two weeks, I cut 60 fingernails and toenails—sometimes 80 (if I help Ian), and sometimes 100 if I do mine. And now as of July 2, 2015, I can add 40 more nails to the workload. Yes, the floor is a mess. So whenever I am gearing up for the task, I grab our handheld vacuum. I cut everyone's nails and then vacuum up the mess. So simple.

Emergency Contact

We should all have an Emergency Contact List posted in our homes. I remember my mom had one when we were growing up, and instead of tucking it away, she put it in a nice frame and hung it on the wall above the phone. Wherever you decide to have one is fine—just make one. Show your sitters, kids, and guests where it is. Here is some helpful information for your list:

- Your home address in BIG, BOLD letters
- Your contact info (work phone, email, cell phone, etc.)
- Nearest hospital
- Medical information about your family
- Neighbors' names, addresses, and contact numbers
- Emergency contacts (at least three)
- Children's schools and addresses

- Each child's height, weight, eye color, and birth date
- Other information can include: service numbers (yard, plumbing, cleaning, electric, furnace, A/C, appliance repair, water company, electric company, gas company, alarm company, locksmith, etc.)

Plastic Bag

Sitting on an airplane is cramped; there are no two ways about it. Added with the garbage from drinks and snacks, you end up having no room at all. Your tray ends up filled with drinks and food containers, so you can't reach anything in the bag stored under the seat in front of you. Sometimes the pocket in front of you is filled up with garbage, so you can't pull your tray down. Forget getting up to use the loo after mealtime, because you have to wait for the flight attendant to come get your trash. Bottom line: it's crammed.

Don't worry, I have a solution. Next time you fly (and this goes for long car rides too), bring a tall kitchen drawstring garbage bag with you (one for each leg of your trip). While you are in the plane, you always have a place for your trash. Make sure your bag has a drawstring so you can cinch it up. You can put the bag anywhere under your feet and it doesn't matter if you step on it. You have a great place for your trash, and you don't have to wait for the flight attendant. At the end of your flight, you can leave the bag in your seat or carry it off the plane and dispose of it yourself. Trust me, this is great.

I also keep a roll of plastic bags in the car. You never know when someone is going to have an accident, get carsick, have muddy soccer gear, etc.

Kids' Artwork

Have you ever been caught throwing away your kids' artwork? I have! A piece of paper I think looks like someone checking to see if a pen works has a full story. ("I made it for Daddy at school when Lacey was teaching, but now it's for Harvey" or "It's a treehouse; it's for you, do you love it?") I average 20 pieces of art from the kids at home and then probably 50 projects from school a week. It's a lot, and like any good mommy, I want to keep it all (kinda). But like any good mommy, I wonder where I am going to put it all.

I know there are those super parents who scan it all, pay the $50 bucks every three months, and have books and books of their children's art "published." That ain't happening for me; I'm too cheap. And way, way too impatient to scan artwork. I love, love, love my children and their art, but I had to come up with a system to manage it. Here is what I do:

1. I let the kids put anything and everything up on the walls in their rooms. No, my children's rooms will *not* be photographed for a Land of Nod advertisement, but my kids are happy. And they can tell you a story about each piece and where they made it and how. In my room, I keep a roll of that blue tape used for painting, and when they want to hang something, they come and ask for tape.
2. I have a bin under each of the children's beds for their artwork. At the end of the year, we can go through it together. Maybe some goes on the wall in their rooms, maybe some goes to family members, and the rest goes in the recycling bin.

3. I only keep what I like. I'm going to be the one oohing and aahing over this stuff in ten years. No one else is really going to care much.
4. If something is really amazing, it goes in a frame on the wall.

Thank You, Teachers

Last year Teddy raved about his gym teacher. At the end of the school year, I told Teddy he should draw his gym teacher a picture and write him a note. I explained to him that if you think someone is awesome, you really should let them know, and a great way to do it is to put pen to paper. So we did just that, and he had me thinking. What a great thing for our children to do. They should write thank-you notes to their teachers at the end of the year.

Kids' Socks

Are you tired of losing socks? I am used to it. But if it's driving you crazy, you should purchase a linen bag for each kiddo. Simply have them toss their dirty socks in their own linen bags, and once a week, you can run the bag through the wash. You may need to buy a few extra pairs of socks to get you through the week, but it might be worth it. In our laundry room, I have a bin labeled "missing socks." Whenever I find a single sock, I toss it in the "missing socks" bin. Every few weeks, I have one of the kids dump out the bin and put all the pairs together. Those socks without a pair go in the rag pile.

There Was Once a Diaper at the Park

Okay, so there are always lots of diapers at the park—some mom, dad, or caregiver typically has one. Next time you are at the park and the slide has a puddle at the bottom or the swing is wet, grab a diaper out of your bag, or borrow one from the nearest mommy or nanny, and use it to absorb the puddles. No more wet bums at the park.

2 Great Tips for Kids' PJs

- If your little ones have grown out of their footie pajamas, simply cut the feet off below the zipper. Voila, those pajamas should fit for another three to six months.

- I wrote about this earlier, but in case you forgot: If your little ones like to take their pajamas and diaper off during rest time (and sometimes leave you with a horrible mess), purchase full-zip pajamas—either without feet or cut the feet off—and put them on backwards. They can't reach the zippers and can't get the pajamas off. No more dirty diaper show.

Alarm Clocks for Kids

You already know how I feel about the importance of sleep for kids. Well, it's just as important for me to get my sleep. A friend told me about these great alarm clocks. The brand I bought is by Kid'Sleep, but there are tons of versions. The alarm clock has a little animal (bunny/cow/cat). When the bunny/cow/cat is lit up and sleeping in a bed, it's time for our children to be quiet in their beds, hopefully sleeping. If the bunny/cow/cat wakes up and plays, then our children are allowed to get out of their beds too. It's great; our alarms are set for the bunny/cow/cat to sleep from 7:00 p.m., when our kids go to bed, to 7:00 a.m., when our children can come out of their rooms. So unless someone is sick or has an accident, we do not hear from our children from 7:00 a.m. to 7:00 p.m.

Yes, we are very lucky. We have twelve hours each day to ourselves. Our children are even luckier because they each have twelve guaranteed hours of sleep at night. It took a lot to train the kids to learn, understand, and accept the alarm clocks, and it took even more training to get David on board, but we got there. Here's how we did it:

1. We got Teddy his clock before he was two years old. We ended up getting Harvey's and Wiggy's alarms a bit earlier.

2. We put the clocks in their rooms. When we put them to bed, we would have the clock set so the bunny/cow/cat was sleeping. And we would say, "Your bunny is sleeping; it's bedtime for you too. Time to go to sleep." We said it religiously every night and made sure they looked at the clocks.

3. In the morning, if they called for us (remember, our children stayed in their cribs until age four), we would go into their rooms, and the first thing (before we said good morning) was, "Did your bunny play?" They would look at their clock and say yes or no. If the answer was no, we would say it's not time to get up yet; let me know when your bunny plays. If they needed it, we would tuck them back in, say goodnight, and leave the room. And, yes, our children would SCREAM! But since they were either in the basement or on the third floor, it didn't disturb anyone.

4. Now everyone is pretty much trained up. From time to time, we have to talk about the bunny/cow/cat. We don't have the alarms set to make sounds; they just light up and we hear our kids yell, "My bunny played!" That's our cue to go in and get them out of their cribs.

At age four, Teddy got a bed. We still used the alarm clock with him. If our kids wake up early (like Teddy normally does), they get great quiet time to themselves. If they sleep in, even better. The goal has always been to keep our household nice and quiet until 7:00 a.m., and it is.

Double Sheets

All of our children's beds have four sheets on them. The first sheet is the mattress protector, the second sheet is a regular fitted sheet, the third sheet is a mattress protector, and the fourth sheet is a regular fitted sheet. At 3:00 a.m., when someone has an accident, all we (or our child) have to do is strip off the first two layers of the sheets (the regular sheet and the mattress protector) and our child can hop back in dry bedding without much work.

Kids' Athletic Gear

I started this with Ian ten years ago. Ian spends half of his time with us and half of his time with his mom. I purchased three drawstring backpacks so Ian could keep his gear organized and schlep it from house to house easily. I labeled each bag with his name and one of his sports (soccer, basketball, or baseball). I patiently trained him to put his gear back in its corresponding bag after each use. Uniforms were not put in his dresser drawers from the laundry; they were put back in the proper sport backpack. Today Ian still uses this system, as do the rest of our children.

Disposable Cups

Ladies and gentlemen—keep a stack of these babies in your car, and you will think, "How did I ever live without them?" Here's why:

- Your kids are thirsty. I always have water in the car, but it's a huge jug, not a kid-friendly jug. I pull out one of my disposable cups and share my water.
- Your kids are hungry. If you buy individual packs of pretzels or peanuts, it will cost you $10. If you buy one huge bag, divide the contents into the cups you keep in your car, you save $8 and most likely have leftovers.
- If you find a drinking fountain that barely works, you have cups handy. Fill those babies up.
- You stop for ice cream. You decide to hop in the car before everyone has finished their cones. The kid in the third row says he doesn't want any more ice cream—oh, and I failed to mention it's 95 degrees out. Throw the cone in the cup—zero mess.
- You run out of windshield wiper cleaner on a road trip. You buy a jug at the gas station. You can easily pour it into your car with your cup.
- You go to the beach and don't have the perfect sand-castle-building set. No worries, you got something better: cups! Go ahead and drink the ocean water, kids, cuz mom brought cups!

I am sure there are a lot of other reasons for keeping disposable cups in your car.

A Permanent Marker

I keep a few permanent markers in my car. One summer, with three small children in tow, we went to our first carnival. I had taken one child to a fair before, but taking all three seemed like a science experiment for losing children. So as we were getting out of the car, I got out my permanent marker. I wrote my phone number on each of my kids' hands. If they got lost, I knew someone would see the number, because it was *very* visible. The kids also knew they had my number "tattooed" on them. Yes, it's kinda crazy, and I think David was kinda embarrassed. But you never know. And I know this is not a sure-fire way to get a child returned, but it was better than nothing.

There are other reasons to keep a permanent marker in your car:

- You can write anyone a note, and if you have to leave it in the rain, the note won't get ruined.
- If you need to label anything (kids' uniforms, sports equipment, etc.), you are ready.
- You can even label a disposable cup.

Flip-Flops, Keens, and Crocs

All these cute little shoes need to be cleaned. Just throw all your family members' rubber sandals right in the dishwasher, put the soap in the dispenser, and press "Start." All your summer shoes come out spotless. Here is a list of other items I run through the dishwasher.

- Light fixtures.
- Lunch boxes.
- Baseball hats.
- Cup holder inserts from my car.
- Small coolers.
- Bath toys.

- Hair brushes.
- Dog dishes.
- Waste baskets.
- Refrigerator shelves and drawers.
- Silverware organizers.

Chiffonier, Bureau, Highboy, Dresser, Cabinet, Wardrobe, Etc.

One night, I walked into Teddy's room, and he had every single drawer in his dresser pulled open. Thankfully I mounted his dresser to the floor so it would tip over on him.

Not to freak you out, but just to make you aware, dressers or any large furniture falling on children is a big cause for injury and death for little ones. This website—www.meghan-shope.org—is dedicated to raising awareness about this issue. The mother who created it lost her little one when her dresser toppled on her.

You don't have to totally freak out about this, but do consider some way to mount heavy furniture. As you know, little ones will figure out *any* method to climb something, *especially* to get something they "need."

Smoke Detectors

A fireman told me this rule: every time you change your clocks (forward or backwards), change the batteries in your smoke detectors. At the same time, use an aerosol air gun, and blow all the dust out of your smoke detectors.

Clean Your Car in Public

The next time you get out of the car, grab all the trash—empty cups, garbage, anything you don't need—and throw it in the nearest garbage can. It's best to do this when you are out in public, because there is always a garbage can close by. And when you are getting out of your car at home, you are most likely grabbing your gym bag, shopping bags, dry cleaning, etc.—in other words, your hands are already full. When you get out of your car away from your house, you generally don't have much in your hands, and there is always a trash bin nearby.

Doctor's Appointments

Everyone is pretty healthy at our house, but we still have a lot of doctor's and dentist's appointments to schedule and keep track of. I have figured out a great trick to keep everyone's appointments on track. We all go for our annual doctor's and dentist's appointments around our birthdays. Yeah, I know: Happy Birthday, you have a cavity! HAHAHA. But it's so easy this way. When a birthday is coming up, not only do I start buying birthday gifts and planning birthday parties, I also schedule doctor's and dentist's appointments. And to keep the dentist's appointment scheduling simple, I make sure I schedule the next dentist's appointment at each appointment, to make sure our teeth are checked every six months. Get your family on this schedule, and you will wonder how you did it any other way.

Doctor's appointments are a one-kid operation. You really want to focus on one kid at time. And the doctor likes it better this way too. Just ask a friend to watch your other kids.

And one more thing, if you have questions for your children's doctor or your own doctor, make sure you keep a list of them on the date of the visit in your calendar.

Gesundheit or Salud or Prosit

Before the cold and flu season commences, get your home prepared. Make sure you are ready and stocked up on the following so you are prepared:

- Vitamin C.
- Emergen-C—there are flavors for everyone in your family.
- Cold and flu tea or your favorite tea.
- Probiotics (you should be taking these all the time anyway, but they are really important when you are sick).
- Load up on tissues.
- Load up on hand soap for your bathrooms.
- Get a big supply of paper towels for the puking.
- Load your pantry with chicken noodle soup.
- Load your car with wipes, tissues, and maybe a towel or two for big messes (a couple of garbage sacks are easy to store and pretty handy if you need them).
- Medicine—are all your family favorites up to date (decongestants, fever reducers, etc.)? We don't use medicine; I tend to go the natural route when possible. If that is your family plan too, are you ready? Cold socks, castor oil, heating pads, etc.?

Other things you can do to prepare your house for the cold and flu season:

- Is your thermometer handy and working? I generally don't take the kids' temperatures; I look for other signs to determine if we need medical attention.
- Clean all your blankets so they are ready for the winter.
- Make sure you have extra sheets ready, in case accidents happen.
- Do you have movies, books, puzzles, etc., ready to go for sick days?
- Do you have backup childcare if you need it?
- Do you have some extra sick days at work?
- Do you have cozy pajamas for everyone?
- If your family gets flu shots, have you scheduled to do this?

I know it's a lot, but it's so much easier to have it handy and ready to go now, rather than at three in morning. So get prepared and you will be prepared.

Kids' Medicine

Wiggy got strep when she was three. That was a first for us. Anyway, she was given 10 days of antibiotics. The pharmacy gave us one of those spoon dispensers for her prescription. It wasn't her style; it spilled all over. I was so happy I had saved a small medicine measuring cup and a couple of pharmaceutical plastic syringes from other medications. Those are so much easier—and they make great bath toys too. I always check which dispenser is given with the kids' prescriptions.

No Empty Hands

Do not walk around your house empty-handed. With our busy household, there is always something out of place. So I rarely walk around the house empty-handed. When I leave a room, I do a quick scan and grab anything that does not belong in that particular room and return it to its home.

Here are some examples:

- You are headed to the laundry room; is there anything (dish towels, socks, blankets, jackets, etc.) that needs to be washed? Take it with you.

- You are near your stockpile of toilet paper, paper towels, Ziploc baggies—do these items need to be restocked anywhere in your home? If so, do it.

- You are headed outside for a run or walk; do any of your trash bins need to be emptied? If so, do it.

- You are headed to your car; do you need to replace the tissue, chapstick, permanent marker, plastic bags, diaper stockpile, etc., in your car? Do it now.

- You are headed to your garage; is there anything in your house that needs to be in the garage? If so, grab it and take it there now.

- I also use our laundry bins to move stuff around our house. I had one of those big scrubbers in our upstairs shower. I wanted to get it back to the base-ment where I keep that stuff, so I just threw it in with the dirty laundry. When I loaded the laundry into the machine, there it was, and I put it back in its drawer.

The point is: think before you switch rooms in your house. Obviously, dirt makes a house dirty. Stuff cluttered everywhere makes a house messy. So if you start thinking about getting things in your home back to where they belong, your house will quickly become *very* tidy. When you get up from reading this book, scan the room and grab something that belongs elsewhere and return it to its home.

Storing/Organizing Memories

How do you keep track of *all* the memories not on your computer, in a photo album, or framed hanging on your wall? I'm talking about art projects, ticket stubs, funny things you have written down about your family, invitations you want to hold on to, memories you should write down and store somewhere, love letters, postcards—you get the point. Do you just toss it here or there, or throw it in a box to tackle later?

I have the perfect solution. I call it a memory book. I use one of those large, black, hardcover sketch books; they retail for $12 to $18. They are very durable, and the pages are very thick. I have a book for each of our kids, and one for David and myself. I keep a basket in our basement and I toss all the "memory" stuff in there. When I have a free hour, I go through the basket and tape stuff into their books and write little notes to them about what has been going in on their lives. I have found clear packing tape to be the strongest. The memory books do not look fancy at all. I do them quickly and jot a note or two from time to time. Here are things I tape into their books:

- One or two ultrasound pictures.
- Hair from their first haircut.

- First airline tickets.
- Weight and height graph from their doctor's appointments.
- The first time they wrote their names, drew a smiley face, etc.
- Grades.
- School pictures.
- Funny quotes.
- Favorite foods at various times.
- What they were for Halloween.
- When I am really on the ball, I photocopy their notes to Santa and put them in each kid's book.
- Birthday cards—just a few from special people.
- Every couple of months, I write them a group note telling them what's going on in our lives and their lives. And when I have time or there's a special event, I write an individual note to one kid and put that in that kid's book.
- I also put receipts from various things—toys, food, gas—in their books, because I think it will be interesting for them to see the price of things when they were growing up.

Frozen Pizza

When I make or order pizza, I make or buy extra. I cut the leftovers up into child-sized slices, bag them in Ziploc bags and put them in the freezer. When the children pack their lunches, they often grab frozen pizza from the freezer for the lunches. By the time they sit down for lunch at school, they have a nice cold piece of pizza for lunch.

Vacation and Groceries

In addition to the packing, traveling, flying, driving, laundry, and fun, we also have to eat. So before we return from a trip, I go online with my grocery list (including *easy* meals planned for the week we return) and order all my groceries. I have the groceries delivered the day we return, but before we get home. I arrange for a neighbor or friend to bring in the groceries.

Speaking of Meal Planning

I plan meals. When it was just David, Ian, and me, I would spend $300 per week on groceries. Granted, I was stressed because my mom was so sick; I had a new job, new marriage, and new stepson; we had just bought our first house together; and I was pregnant—but still, for a family of three, $300 per week was a lot of money! I knew from school that meal planning was a cost-effective way to eat, and that it was often healthier. So I started meal planning our dinners. I planned the basics for breakfast and lunch, and then planned our dinners around what I had time to cook, our schedule, and the weather. In the beginning, I kept it pretty simple—every night I had a plan for our dinner table. I never had to worry about what we were going to eat for dinner. If I had a free moment in the morning, I could start our meal preparations. Meal planning decreased our grocery bill, but the real savings came later, when I had our groceries delivered. Our weekly bill went from $300 per week to $100 per week.

How do you start meal planning? Start simple.

1. Pick your six favorite recipes. Or go for the basics: pizza, mac and cheese, tacos, chili, and breakfast for dinner (a huge hit in our house). If you don't cook, pick your six favorite frozen meals, and if you order takeout every night, don't bother meal planning.

2. Look at your calendar and check which nights you will have time to cook. Or, if you have time, start a meal right after school drop-off, or throw everything in the crockpot before you leave for work. You can also do a "big cook" on Sunday night to get you through the week.

3. Build your grocery list. Check all the recipes to see that you have all the ingredients.

4. Go to the grocery store for your groceries—or, like me, have your groceries delivered.

5. I only plan dinner for six nights of the week. Even I need a night off from cooking. That seventh night might be a spread of leftovers, it might be a snack plate, or we might go out.

In the beginning it will be a challenge to stick to your meal plan, and maybe a bit stressful. It's a learning process. Stick with it; after a month you will have the program down and you will be surprised you didn't start it long ago.

Produce Bags

If you do a farm share, I suggest buying a roll of produce bags from your local grocery. It will keep your produce drawer clean and organized. If you are a real do-gooder, purchase those reusable produce bags for your produce.

Family Schedule

This is a good follow-up to meal planning. You are always going to get caught off guard with your family schedule. Get used to it.

Your family schedule (or lack thereof) is going to get messed up all the time. Mine does and I just do the best I can. And if you are reading this book, you are probably the person in charge of the doctor's appointments, house maintenance, grocery shopping, dinner, laundry, driving, school schedule, etc. Get your family on a schedule now. You are much less likely to be chasing your tail all week. And when things get messed up, it's much easier to recover.

Every Sunday night I do our family schedule, meal plan, babysitter schedule, and grocery order. In the beginning, it took me about two hours to decide what we were eating for dinner, make our grocery list, look at everyone's activities, plug in babysitters and carpooling where we might need them. Now, with lots of practice, I can whip out our weekly schedule in about 30 minutes.

I highly, highly recommend making a family schedule if you have found yourself upside down because you have family members heading every different direction. When I do the schedule on Sunday night, I get a glimpse into what our week is going to be like. This also gives me a chance to plan dinner meals based on the amount of time, or lack thereof, we have on a specific day. If I see in the schedule I can't give a kid a ride somewhere, I can organize a carpool early. I also get a chance to look at the rest of the month and keep tabs on what we have going on. Here is an example of our family schedule:

Monday	Tuesday	Wednesday	Thursday	Friday	Saturday	Sunday
Harvey NO SCHOOL David out of town Ian with us Teddy, Wiggy & Harvey Art @ 3:30PM	Ian with us Bring Snacks to Wiggy's class Teddy, Wiggy & Harvey 3:15PM Tennis 4:00PM Teddy (optional) soccer practice 6:30PM - 9:00PM Ian soccer practice David out of town	Ian late opening Ian with Kristen Wiggy and Teddy early dismissal 2:30PM Date Night put garbage out 10:00AM Harvey doc appt	Teddy, Wiggy, Harvey Tennis @ 3:15PM Kysa meeting 7:00PM Ian with Kristen 10:00AM furnace fixed	Ian with us Wiggy and Teddy early dismissal @ 11:30AM Dinner with the Smith family Take Ian to get his eyes checked 2:45PM	Ian with us 8:00AM (be there at 7:30) Teddy soccer game Wilcox Field #2 8:00AM Harvey and Wiggy soccer Practice 10:00AM Wiggy Birthday Party for Amy (no gifts) 2:00PM (be there at 1:15) Ian soccer tourney in Beaverton 5:00PM lecture at the zoo take all the kids 7:00PM grocery delivery	Ian with us 2 Hours of Chores..... vacuum cars, tidy up garage, clean out junk food drawer, clean out fridge & freezer, weed ALL beds, sweep porch, remove cobwebs and spider webs around porches, clean out take the kids swimming
Babysitter	**Babysitter** 2:30PM - 9:00PM	**Babysitter** 7:00PM - 10:00PM	**Babysitter**	**Babysitter**	**Babysitter**	**Babysitter**
Dinner	**Dinner**	**Dinner**	**Dinner**	**Dinner**	**Dinner**	**Dinner**
Tacos sliced oranges carrots	Spaghetti Salad	Breakfast for Dinner!	Snack Plate - cheese, crackers, grapes, almonds, celery french bread and cucumber sandwiches	Going out to eat	Pasta Carbonara Asparagus	BBQ Steak Mashed potato Mushrooms in garlic butter Sliced tomato

60 Minutes

Pick a day every week and set the timer in your home for one hour (we do two hours). This hour is dedicated to everyone contributing to helping around the house. It's **FAMILY CHORE HOUR**. I keep a list in my calendar of all the chores I want done around the house. When the weekend comes, I delegate the chores out to everyone in the family. Be creative—and remember, this is a great way to teach your kids how to take care of their future homes, learn new skills, and contribute to the household. Here is a list of chores to help you get started:

- Go through a bucket of markers and check to see which work and which don't.
- Go through a bucket of toys and toss the broken parts.
- Sweep.
- Match socks in a missing sock bin.
- Empty garbage cans.
- Clean toilets.
- Re-stock paper supplies around the house.
- Pull weeds.
- Clean bikes.
- Sort shoes.
- Dust.
- Clean out the fridge and pantry.
- Empty everything out of drawers in the kitchen, wipe the drawers clean, and put everything back.
- Change light bulbs.

Sprinklers + Soap

I love summer. But after cooking dinner and cleaning the kitchen, I'm tired and hot. I don't want to go upstairs, where it's hotter, to help the kids with their showers. So I have our little ones strip down to their birthday suits in the back yard, turn the sprinkler timer on for 30 minutes, and let them run wild. I grab a large tote bag and fill it with soap, shampoo, toothbrushes, toothpaste, towels, pajamas, pull-ups, and diapers, and bring it all outside. The kids fill up their baby pool, play soccer, go down the plastic kiddie slide; they go nuts running through the sprinklers. I sit back with a cocktail and watch the show. As the playing winds down, I slip in and wash their bodies and hair and have them brush teeth during all the fun. When the sprinklers go off, it's time for pajamas and bed. I fill the tote bag up with everything and we head inside for books and bed.

Live in 30-Minute Increments

When Wiggy was born, my life slowed way, way down. I had two infants and a nine-year-old. And with a C-section, I wasn't allowed to drive for six weeks. So we were homebound. We would get up, have breakfast, and then head to the basement, where most of the toys were. It got boring very quickly, but I was tied to home. I had to spice it up, I was going nuts. In the morning, I would make a mental plan for the day in 30-minute increments. The goal was to get my stuff done and get Teddy involved where I could. We would have breakfast for 30 minutes, head to the basement for 30 minutes (I would breastfeed Murphy), get out markers and paper for 30 minutes (I could also check email), go for a walk for 30 minutes (exercise), go play in one of the kids' rooms for 30 minutes, read books for 30 minutes (I would read one book and let Teddy look at books while I made lunch), and then have lunch. This may seem a little crazy, but it kept us moving around, even if it was just in the house. And it kept me sane. I did not start each day wondering what we were going to do. And now when I am home for the day with the kids and we are having one of those days where there is fighting or someone gets hurt every ten minutes, I quickly come up with a 30-minute plan to keep us busy. To you, it may not seem like a big deal to move around your house, but to your child, it's a whole new world. And, remember, these are perfect opportunities to work with your child on how to clean up. Let's say your next activity is fort building in the bedroom. Tell your child, "We are going to build a fort, but we can't get started until the markers and coloring books are put back in their home."

Book Party

Do you ever see your kids in need of some downtime, but you don't want to turn on the TV for them? Have a book party. Tell them to go round up all their favorite books around the house. Have them bring them wherever you want them to be, or wherever they want to be. Once you have all the books in a big pile in the middle of the room, let your children sit on the floor so they can flip and peruse the books at their own speed.

No, this is not a time for you to read them 20 books. You might need to do a little training here. Sit down with your kids, pick up a book, and look at the pictures. *Do not read a word. Do not tell your children you will not be reading to them* (your children, like all children, will beg for what they cannot have). Instead, focus on the pictures. Point out a few things to get them rolling. Tell your kids you will be right back, step away, get a few things done, come back to check on the party, flip through a book, and step away again. You get the point.

I have done this for a few years with our kids, and they love running around the house gathering books. It takes them a good 20 minutes. And then they plop down and start flipping pages. It's great.

The Bin

Everyone with small children needs a bin. You want to spend 10 minutes with one child to work on the piano, but your other two children will not give you 30 seconds? You want to shower one child and the other one is loose? It's naptime for two of your children and the other one isn't napping anymore? What do you do? You get a bin and you fill it with the best items in your house. And you only pull the bin out when you need 10 to 20 minutes. You never keep the bin out longer than 20 minutes. Seriously—set a timer, and when that timer goes off, you and your child pack up the bin and tuck it away. Tears are okay. If your child is crying because the bin is going away, then you know you have created the best bin.

I used the bin for Harvey when I needed to shower Murphy and Teddy. It was amazing. So what do you put in the bin?

1. Tape measure.
2. Big bolts with nuts on them; I secured a rubber band at the end so the nut couldn't come off.
3. One or two small books.
4. Spatula.
5. Pipe cleaners.
6. Old set of keys on a keychain.
7. Three or four plastic cups.
8. Two or three fun hats.
9. A pair of mom's shoes.

I never put food in the bin. I would swap the toys out constantly. Don't worry; I did not put a lot of effort into this. When I saw something in the house that caught my eye for the bin, I would swap it out for something in the bin. The bin is your secret evolving toy bin; make sure it's always exciting, make sure it's always changing, and you will always get that extra 20 minutes. I will point out, that I only used the bin for one child at a time. If you need to use the bin for two children, I would *highly* suggest two bins. And do not put the two children within eyesight of each other to play with their bins. Separate the children by a bed, counter, door, table, whatever—just separate them. Everyone gets a few minutes to themselves when the bins come out.

Birthday Door

After the children go to sleep the night before their birthdays, we decorate the outside of their bedroom doors. We use streamers and balloons. We have even been known to tape candy and money to their doors. Our children love waking up on their birthdays to check out their decorated doors. They tell us the night before their birthdays to not forget to decorate their doors.

You can have a little fun with your children. One year Ian told us he had an infestation of ladybugs in his room. I phoned the exterminator and he said no one has ever asked to have ladybugs removed. I went up to Ian's room to see if I could figure out where they were coming in. I could only find five ladybugs. I asked if there were more, and he said no, five is a lot. That year I decorated Ian's door with a ladybug theme.

Toothbrushes

Every three months, get new toothbrushes or toothbrush heads. When your bristles aren't straight anymore, they can't clean your teeth as well. You can thank me later for your tiny dentist bill.

Mattresses

Unless you have a mattress that does not need flipping, be sure to flip your mattress every six months. Also, clean your dust ruffle and mattress protector sheet. If you do not have either of these, get them.

Pillows

Your pillows should be cleaned quarterly (every three months). Just pop them in the washing machine (one or two at a time) with a tiny bit of bleach to get the stains out. Dry them with tennis balls (three to four to get the fluff back) in the dryer. This works great for down pillows and okay for synthetics.

Silverware and Kitchen Utensil Drawers

Dump all your silverware onto your counter before you go to bed, run your silverware organizer through the dishwasher overnight. In the morning, dry off any excess water, put it back in your drawer, and put the silverware back in.

Food Expiration Dates

While you are on the phone with your best friend, as I consistently am, clean out your fridge. Take everything out of the fridge, wipe it down, check all expiration dates, and put everything back in the fridge. Next, do your pantry. Do this every three months. And, by the way, ketchup only lasts three months from the date you open it. Yeah, I didn't know that either.

MCH

A year ago, I read *The Astronaut Wives Club* by Lily Koppel. Great book if you need one. Anyway, these women raised their kids and supported their husbands and each other. It is a fabulous book about the astronauts, but also about how women can support each other in this world of childrearing. They often sat around the pool, smoking cigarettes, and enjoying a cocktail or two in the afternoon. So I thought, why in the hell do I even have a witching hour at my house? I should invite some mommies over with their kiddos, open up the bar, and relax. And MCH (Mommy Cocktail Hour) was born. I highly, highly recommend this, ladies and gentlemen.

Here's what I do. I pull out all our liquor, a couple of mixers (whatever is in the fridge), a bucket of ice, and plastic cups. I do not go to the store for anything. This is not a formal event. This is about having a drink before we all start the mad rush of dinner and bedtime. I don't have appetizers or snacks. I sit, my friends sit, and the kids run wild. I put strict hours on my little party—3:30 p.m. to 5:00 p.m.— and my friends know me; if they don't offer to leave, I will escort them to the door when I need them to go. After sitting around for an hour and a half with my friends, I have a light buzz and tired kids, and I make a simple dinner and tuck my little ones in bed.

That's all, folks. Thank you for reading.

Acknowledgments

I would like to thank the following people for their opinions,
help with grammar, and suggestions.

David Kelleher
Sheena Portrait
Kathleen Helmer
Jennifer Yamin
Kathryn Williams
Catherine Glavan
Kristen LaBarca
Dr. Amy Marr
Allison Williams
Lindsay Donovan
Eloise Koehler
Dr. Sarah Johnson
Gulgun Mersereau
Assistant Principal Teresa Seidel
Heather Matteri
Kathleen Dennison
Alyssa Biniak

CPSIA information can be obtained
at www.ICGtesting.com
Printed in the USA
FSOW02n0452101216
28222FS